RABELAIS

RABELAIS

A Dramatic Game in Two Parts
taken from the Five Books of
François Rabelais
by
JEAN-LOUIS BARRAULT

Translated from the French by
ROBERT BALDICK

 HILL & WANG   *New York*

The halftone photographs in this book are by Photo Pic, Paris. They show rehearsals and scenes from the original Paris production of *Rabelais*.

Rabelais is an author to be drunk, to be savoured by the palate. He is best enjoyed aloud, for his is the acme of the spoken style.

LÉON DAUDET

He led the life of all the great thinkers of his time, an uneasy, wandering, fugitive life, the life of a poor hare between two furrows.

MICHELET

I am a man, and nothing human is alien to me. I have all man's vices and all man's virtues. I understand them, and, taking them upon myself, I am ready to excuse them and forgive them. . . .

TERENCE

DARE!

FRANÇOIS I

Rabelais was first produced at the Élysée-Montmartre, Paris, on 12th December 1968, by the Compagnie Renaud-Barrault.

The cast was as follows:

Marie-Hélène Dasté	WITCH PANZOUST—GRIMALKIN JUSTICE
Dora Doll	GARGAMELLE—ABBEY OF THELEMA— PRINCESS BACBUC

and, in alphabetical order:

Jacques Alric	GRANDGOUSIER—GRIMALKIN
Georges Audoubert	FRIAR JOHN OF THE FUNNELS
Marie-Christine Auferil	LADY-IN-WAITING—LANTERN
Jean-Louis Barrault	ORATOR OF THE COMPANY
Victor Béniard	PILLOT—EUSTHENES
Jean-Pierre Bernard	PANTAGRUEL
Pierre Bertin	OLD GARGANTUA—QUAVERING FRIAR
Gérard Boucaron	YOUNG GARGANTUA—MONK
Vélérie Camille	MARGUERITE OF NAVARRE—QUEEN OF LANTERNLAND
Huguette Dathane	LADY-IN-WAITING—LANTERN
Del Vitto	MONK
Paul Descombes	PONOCRATES—EPISTEMON
Anke Everdine	SINGING ABBESSITE—DANCER—LANTERN
Pierre Gallon	DUNGHILL—XENOMANES
Jean-Renaud Garcia	FARMER—SAILOR—TAXALOT
Philippe Gauguet	GYMNAST
Jean-Pierre Granval	PLAY-LEADER

9

Louis Frémont	SHEPHERD FROGIER—CARPALIM
Jean-Pierre Jorris	PICROCHOLE—TRIBOULET—THE BEGGAR
Hubert de Lapparent	TOUCHFAUCET—AEDITUS
Jean Moussy	MARQUET—CALVIN—DANCER
Régis Outin	THUBAL HOLOFERNES—PUTHERBEUS
Émilie Pareze-Belda	LADY-IN-WAITING—LANTERN
Céline Salles	LADY-IN-WAITING—LANTERN
Dominique Santarelli	EARLYPEAR—DINGDONG
Frank Valois	FRIAR JOHN—WRESTLER
Henri Virlojeux	PANURGE
Jacky Wiecz	TREPELU—WRESTLER

Costumes and décor by Matias
Music by Michel Polnareff
Choreography by Vélérie Camille

Rabelais was presented by the Compagnie Renaud-Barrault for a season at the National Theatre, opening on 24th September 1969.

The cast was as follows:

Vélérie Camille	MARGUERITE OF NAVARRE—QUEEN OF LANTERNLAND
Marie-Hélène Dasté	WITCH PANZOUST—GRIMALKIN JUSTICE
Huguette Dathane	DANCER—LANTERN
Sharon O'Connell	DANCER—SINGING ABBESSITE
E. Pareze-Belda	DANCER—LANTERN
Michèle Rimbold	DANCER—LANTERN
Céline Salles	DANCER—LADY-IN-WAITING TO GARGAMELLE
Jacqueline Staup	PRINCESS BACBUC—GARGAMELLE
Anne Ziegler	DANCER—LANTERN
Jacques Alric	GRANDGOUSIER—GRIMALKIN
Georges Audoubert	FRIAR JOHN OF THE FUNNELS
Jean-Louis Barrault	ORATOR OF THE COMPANY—PONOCRATES—EPISTEMON
Victor Béniard	PILLOT—BEGGAR
Jean-Pierre Bernard	PANTAGRUEL
Fernand Berset	OLD GARGANTUA—QUAVERING FRIAR
Gérard Boucaron	YOUNG GARGANTUA—BACCHUS
Richard Caron	GYMNAST
Claude del Vitto	MONK
Louis Frémont	SHEPHERD FROGIER—CARPALIM
Pierre Gallon	DUNGHILL—XENOMANES
Jean-Renaud Garcia	FARMER—SAILOR—TRIBOULET
Jean-Pierre Granval	PLAY-LEADER—PICROCHOLE

Hubert de Lapparent	TOUCHFAUCET—AEDITUS
Régis Outin	THUBAL HOLOFERNES—PUTHERBEUS
Dominique Santarelli	EARLYPEAR—DINGDONG
Frank Valois	FRIAR JOHN—WRESTLER
Bernard Vignal	TREPELU—WRESTLER
Henri Virlojeux	PANURGE

Production by Jean-Louis Barrault

Designed by Matias
Music by Michel Polnareff
Choreography by Vélérie Camille

Preface

Faith, hope and charity are, it is true, three divine virtues. But I would add that sublime virtue, rare even among the Saints, which, for want of a better name, I would call JOY.

MICHELET

Rabelais has always been an object of predilection for me, for in him I see the Ancestor. The feeling I have for him is something more than admiration. Every time I sink my teeth into him, my mouth is filled with such a savoury juice, my blood is enriched by such a powerful accretion, my spine is strengthened by such a vigorous sap, that I give vent to what he would have called "horrific" cries of enthusiasm.

For Rabelais is Childhood grasping hold of life in both hands.

Is my reaction a sort of peasant atavism? Perhaps. Biologically speaking, I feel very French, and nobody is more French than Rabelais, in either defects or qualities, weakness or genius.

That is probably why, for four centuries, right-minded folk, representing what Michelet called "the mediocre ideal of French common sense", have done their best, if not to kill him off, at least to hide him away as a monster likely to cause the family some embarrassment.

But Rabelais, as a skilled physician, knew that mental constipation produces headaches which are just as painful as those which come from its visceral equivalent. On the other hand, he also knew that joy "comforts and cures the sick and the afflicted".

> *Without health, life is not life, life is not livable.*
> *Without health, life is but languor,*
> *Life is but an image of death.*
> *So you who have no health, and thus are dead,*
> *Seize hold of life, for life is health.*

To reach Rabelais, at least three barriers have to be overcome: Malherbe's austerity, Ronsard's frivolity, and Rabelais's own archaic language.

Sharing as we do Rabelais's universal liberalism, we shall make no attempt to criticize either Malherbe, whose restrictions gave rise to such great beauty, or Ronsard, whose indescribable charm we are the first to admire, as exemplified in such lines as these:

> *Quand au temple nous serons*
> *Agenouillés, nous ferons*
> *Les dévots selon la guise*
> *De ceux qui pour louer Dieu*
> *Humbles se courbent au lieu*
> *Le plus secret de l'Église*
>
> *Mais quand au lit nous serons*
> *Entrelacés, nous ferons*
> *Les lascifs selon la guise*
> *Des amants qui librement*
> *Pratiquent folâtrement*
> *Dans les draps cent mignardises. . .*[1]

Beside Malherbe's royal gilt, which transformed grandeur into pomp, and Ronsard's crumpled sheets, between which the poet "shed lustre on the French language", there is Rabelais's earthiness. There is his immense inspiration, his total freedom, his delirious imagination, his colossal effervescence.

Michelet, whom we have drawn on to a great extent in the present work, once declared: "The essential genius of every nation, its innermost spirit, lies above all in its language."

It was in an attempt to lay bare the "innermost spirit" that three years ago I decided to plunge into Rabelais.

It was a difficult task. To modernize his language is to extinguish it, to betray it. But to leave it buried in the often impenetrable

---

[1] When we are kneeling in our place of worship, we shall play the pious in the manner of those who to praise God bow down humbly in the most secret place in the Church.

But when we are entwined in bed, we shall play the lechers in the manner of those lovers who freely indulge in countless frolicsome practices between the sheets.

undergrowth of archaism is to refuse to bring it within reach of our modern ears.

I have to recognize here that the idea of this undertaking was first given to me by the excellent Magnard edition of Rabelais's works, thanks to the text established by Monsieur Roger Delbiausse and Marcel Aymé's perceptive introduction.

This obstacle of Rabelais's language has proved to be the most delicate part of my work, and will probably be the most vulnerable to criticism from the experts.

What tempted me most of all was the chance of bringing out the dramatic quality of this great author who left us his situations and his dialogue, so to speak, "in the rough".

The idea of Rabelais as a dramatist is not a new one. It has already been put forward by Léon Daudet, among other writers. And this is not the first time the Picrocholine War has been put on the stage.[1]

However, in order to remain faithful to Rabelais and paint a portrait bearing some resemblance to him, the enterprise had to be utterly mad. Rabelais had to be taken in his entirety. A play had to be drawn from his five books, from his letters, from his prophecies —from his Complete Works.

I have tried to avoid the aridity of the "digest", while combining and concentrating the rich flavours of his writings.

The sacrifices I had to make were cruel, and I still find myself thinking regretfully and angrily of certain sublime chapters I had to leave out.

What else could I do? If I had kept only the scatalogical passages I would have made him nothing but a medico; the erotic passages, nothing but a lecherous monk; the gastronomic passages, nothing but a drunkard; the evangelical passages, nothing but a more or less apostate priest.

Rabelais is all that, and much more besides.

He is a Tree. Its roots suck up clay and dung. Its trunk is as stiff as a phallus. Its foliage is encyclopaedic (the word comes from him). Its blossoms shoot up to God.

[1] Léon Chancerel produced a dramatic version of the war some twenty years ago. Students at the Sorbonne put on an excellent production of it recently.

Rabelais does not live turned in upon himself: he looks out towards the world. An eternal student, irreverent, obstinate, cunning and restless, his temperament leads him, despite his loyalty to tradition, to take his place among those fighting for new ideas.

That is the modest point of contact we have with him.

From the pleasant garden of France he ventures into space. In his Chinon cellar, between two draughts of "Septembral juice", he thinks of interplanetary journeys. He foresees the exploration of space, from Jules Verne to Gagarin. And his times are our times.

Through the great discoveries, Magellan's Asia and the America of Columbus and Jacques Cartier, space is enlarged. Through the invention of printing, antiquity returns from exile and the means of communication are extended. As soon as the scale of communications is enlarged, human society undergoes a change. Civilizations enter into conflict or are brought into harmony. Asia is found to have its own morality, the East is discovered to be just as holy as the West, and mankind is seen to be *identical*. There is a return to Nature, revolution, contestation, schism.

Politics spread into new areas. The police become a weapon of the State.

The parallels between our two periods are obvious.[1]

But where others have recourse to cruelty and oppression, Rabelais joins the side of *tolerance*.

Three forces are in play. The first is Catholicism, holding up the march of History or trying to adapt itself to it by shedding its Christian elements. The second is Protestantism which, on the contrary, seizes hold of History and tries to plant Christian purity in it once more. And the third is the humanism of Erasmus, of Guillaume Budé, of Lefèvre d'Étaples ... of Rabelais, who in desperation devote themselves to the cause of universal reconciliation.

Young François I and his sister Marguerite of Navarre are the heroes of the enterprise. The England of Henry VIII will be the beneficiary.

At Marignano in 1515, after Francois's great victory, the future looks bright. But at Pavia ten years later, with François defeated and taken prisoner, the skies are dark with clouds. Gargantua is

[1] It was a complete coincidence that I finished writing this work just before the events of May 1968.

born in the joy of victory, Pantagruel in the despondency of defeat and captivity.

The bankers of the world step in. Gold pours into Europe from America. The terror of the Inquisition, elaborated by Loyola, is set in motion thanks to Charles V, *alias* Picrochole. And Panurge has to sail away to avoid being burnt at the stake.

This is a period of tribulation. The Wars of Religion are not far away.

What is to be done? Is man to give himself up to the pessimism of an Albrecht Dürer: "The present is bad, but the future is worse. And the clock that I see will strike only evil hours"? NO! In spite of everything: DRINK OF LIFE!

Be your own judge of what you do. Life is not a matter of taking or receiving but of extending and giving. "To reach the end of the road of knowledge, take God as your guide and man as your companion."

And lastly, bear in mind this dictum which is so important to us today:

Do as you will because people are free.

A terrifying dictum because of the various interpretations which can be placed upon it. Our own conviction on this subject is as follows:

In order to be *entirely free*, man must construct a system of morals for himself. Without such a system, freedom is limited. But if that system of morals is not to restrict the horizons of freedom, if on the contrary it is to open every window wide to it, then it can only be based on the noblest of all human feelings: *the spirit of charity*. Charity taken in the etymological sense of the word: to cherish or love.

Love your neighbour as yourself.

On that point all the world's religions are in agreement. It is also the credo of the free-thinker.

Once that has been accepted, man rediscovers his original purity: a childlike nature, a metaphysical ease, an innate courtesy.

Rabelais is essentially a pure being.

His childlike nature entitles him to every sort of excess, his familiarity with religion to every sort of criticism and fantasy, his innate courtesy to every sort of audacity and humour.

He was born seventy years before Shakespeare. His work, when it is studied with care, is seen to be skilfully constructed. We hope that the "dramatic game" we have taken from it will remind the reader or playgoer of Molière, La Fontaine, Alfred Jarry, Aristophanes, Kafka, the Renaissance, the circus of all periods and . . . our own times.

Rabelais has often been described as immense, enormous, protean. But what humanity there is in him too, what true poetry!

An insatiable hunger for knowledge, sex, refinement. A frantic love of life.

JEAN-LOUIS BARRAULT
September 1968

PART ONE

Gargantua and Pantagruel

Prologue I[1]

*A few minutes before the performance begins, the members of the
orchestra come into the auditorium in their own time and start tuning
up, playing snatches of classical or contemporary music.*

*The actors arrive in their turn, carrying costumes or props, like
spectators before a match. Everybody goes about his business quite
naturally, the actors and musicians mingling with the audience as they
take their seats.*

Suddenly a gong is sounded.

A single actor is standing on the stage;[2] this is the Orator.

Ladies and Gentlemen,
Reviving one of the oldest traditions of the theatre, especially the
theatre of the strolling players, I have the honour of speaking to
you tonight as the Orator of our Company.
In similar circumstances I have often had occasion to invoke the
Present Moment. . . . What I mean is. . . .
(*The Orator falls silent, as if suffering from a lapse of memory. The
audience, puzzled, stop moving, freeze, hold their breath. Silence
fills the theatre. After a long, uneasy pause the Orator continues*):
I would like you to realize what is happening just now. I stopped
talking, I stopped making a noise, and suddenly silence took
hold of us. Thanks to that silence we can become aware of the
Reality of the Present, the Reality of Life, of Life in progress.
Reality we can see and feel and touch.
Here we are—you, my fellow actors and I—gathered together in
this theatre, among these walls, playbills, spars and spotlights,
your faces, *our* breath. Outside is our town, then the country.

---

[1] This prologue was not used in the Élysée-Montmartre production. See
Prologue II.

[2] Which is in the shape of a cross, in the middle of the audience.

Beyond that, Europe, and then the World, with its infinite noises, a seething cauldron of news and information. Eurovision. Mondovision. Ebbing and flowing. Accelerating and braking. A jostling of ideas.

Here we are caught between Reaction and Progress; there between sclerosis and permanent revolution. Somewhere else, a new Gospel is being written. In one place, a worn-out war is coming to an end. In another, a new war is being organized. Politics are becoming so complex it is often hard to understand them. The Police are everywhere: in uniform, in plain clothes, and even in the sky, in satellites.

The world is changing: a marvellous, exciting process, but a process that causes fear, disappointment, even boredom. It is a world of such astonishing contrasts and contradictions that nothing else interests us today; a world so absorbing that nothing matters to us that isn't immediately relevant.

Yet this is the moment we choose to show you RABELAIS! Why? Because Rabelais's times are our times. . . .

(Here the Orator is interrupted by his fellow actors who gradually crowd on to the stage, forming at least four groups: the Reactionaries, the Progressives, the Humanists and the Rebels. The following dialogue should be shared out according to the actors' temperaments. The rhythm is accelerando.)

—— Magellan. Christopher Columbus. Jacques Cartier.

—— With the discovery of the New World, space on earth changes its form.

—— With Copernicus, space in the sky changes its appearance.

—— But there are also discoveries made in MAN.

—— Just as we in our day have seen the first heart transplant, Rabelais carried out the first dissection of a corpse.

—— With the discovery of Printing, Time is opened up as well as Space.

—— Knowledge is spread abroad.

—— Information is exchanged.

—— And an avalanche of Revelation falls upon the world.

—— The Spirit of Discovery penetrates even into the mind.

—— Emancipation. A thirst for freedom. A revolt. A return to Nature. A RENAISSANCE.

—— But the emancipation must be contained! The revolt must be crushed!

—— Politics become more sophisticated. This is the age of Machiavelli.

—— The Police become the principal weapon of the State. This is the age of Ignatius Loyola.

—— Bureaucracy, that everlasting parasite, sinks its teeth into society.

—— Money, in the shape of American gold, gives the bankers power.

—— Rabelais's times, or ours?

—— The thirst for knowledge is aroused. Nothing will ever quench it.

—— The spirit of revolt kindles.

—— The spirit of repression hardens.

—— The Western world splits in two.

—— In three!

—— The Pope. Erasmus. Luther.

—— Musicians! Gladiators!

—— Reformers! Papists! Evangelists!

—— Communists! Capitalists! Deviationists!

—— Rabelais's times, or ours?

—— Civil wars. Wars of religion.

—— Trials. Persecutions.

—— Strangling, burning, torturing.

—— Hanging, drawing, quartering.

—— Extermination camps. Re-education camps.

—— Our times, or Rabelais's?

—— Eight hundred thousand Jews are driven out of Spain. Barbarossa saves seventy thousand at one blow!

—— A Barbarian! But what about Pizarro? And what about Cortés? And the slave traffic? And the massacre of the Indians?

—— Rabelais's times! Our times!

—— Men living on the run, hunted like animals.

—— His times or ours: men are as cruel as ever, and the end of the world as close as ever.

—— Between those two calamities called Order and Disorder,

Rabelais, like all the great humanists, belongs to the party of Tolerance. That has always been the minority party. Excommunicated by one side, rejected by the other, what is man to do? Lose heart? Despair? Never!

If we, like Rabelais, have enough childlike simplicity in us, enough religious feeling, enough faith in MAN, then "the others" belong to an absurd world, a comical world, and *in ourselves* astonishment at *being alive* produces a strange feeling which, for want of a better word, we shall call JOY.

———— Joy and the absurd!

(*An Instrument starts playing.*)

A COMIC ACTOR: Listen to my prophecy:

This year, the blind won't see much,

The deaf won't hear much,

The dumb won't speak much,

The rich will be better off than the poor,

The people will suffer from the soldiery,

And God will be all-powerful.

A WOMAN: And there will be more wormwood than usual, and choke-pears and bitter oranges.

A PESSIMIST (*the instrument has stopped playing*): The present is bad, but the future is worse. And the clock that I see will strike only evil hours.

THE HUMANISTS (*reacting violently*):

Without health, life is not life, life is not livable.

Without health, life is but languor,

Life is but an image of death.

So you who have no health, and thus are dead,

Seize hold of life, for life is health.

A QUARTET:

———— When Rabelais came into the world. . . .

———— Joan of Arc had breathed her spirit into France.

———— Three burgher kings had built up France. But France needed a new monarch, a young monarch.

———— Italy awaited his coming. Savonarola had prophesied his coming. Europe itself hoped for his coming.

———— And François I appears at Marignano. A prince of beauty, a flower of youth, a fountainhead of grace and hope.

24

———— He is twenty years old!
  (*A fanfare of trumpets interrupts the quartet.*)
———— Around him are only children:
    Henry VIII is twenty-four!
    Charles V is sixteen!
    Louis of Hungary is only ten!
    The Pope himself is not yet thirty-eight!
———— And behind them, reigning over them, are mothers,
    sisters, aunts, mistresses. Everywhere there is joy and
    laughter, love and licence, mirth and
                    BIRTH!
(*An explosion of noise and gaiety as Gargamelle's Feast begins.*)

Prologue II[1]

While the audience are taking their seats, a huge pile of books is spotlighted in the centre of the cross-shaped stage.

The Orator climbs up on to the side of the cross and strikes a gong to mark the beginning of the performance.

Nine actors enter from all four sides of the cross and gather around the pile of books.

1. (*After striking a huge match, as if to set fire to the books*):
   Society is a sort of prison full of sinners, in which order has to be maintained by force.[2]
2. A free man finds his rule of conduct in his sense of honour.[3]
3. Fear is the foundation of Religion.[4]
4. Fear and slavery pervert human nature.[5]
1. There is not a single drop of good in us and we have no cause to hold ourselves in the slightest regard.[6]
5. Yes, we have: some people have a wonderful gaiety born of a contempt for the quirks of fate.[7] For want of a better name, we call it JOY.[8]
3. God sees nothing in such people but filth and corruption. They are hateful in His sight and He rejects them utterly.[9]
6. I am a man, and nothing human is alien to me. I have all man's vices and all man's virtues. I understand them, and,

[1] This second prologue was used in the Élysée-Montmartre production.
[2] Attributed to Luther (*History of Protestantism*).
[3] Rabelais.
[4] Calvin (*History of Protestantism*).
[5] Rabelais.
[6] Calvin.
[7] Rabelais.
[8] Michelet.
[9] Calvin.

taking them upon myself, I am ready to excuse them and forgive them.[1]

1. Tolerance is licence.[2]
2. Tolerance is a sign of bravery and courage, and often puts a man at a disadvantage.[3]
3. This year[4]. . . .
7. This year, the blind won't see much,
The deaf won't hear much,
The dumb won't speak much,
The rich will be better off than the poor,
The people will suffer from the soldiery,
    And God will be all-powerful.[5]
8. And there will be more wormwood than usual, and choke-pears and bitter oranges.[6]
1. The present is bad, but the future is worse. And the clock that I see will strike only evil hours.[7]
9. Without health, life is not life, life is not livable.
Without health, life is but languor,
Life is but an image of death.
So you who have no health, and thus are dead,
Seize hold of LIFE, for life is health.[8]

(An explosion of music and gaiety as Gargamelle's Feast begins.)

[1] Terence.
[2] *History of Protestantism.*
[3] Marcel Aymé (Introduction to Magnard edition of Rabelais).
[4] Aristotle.
[5] Rabelais (*Prophecies*).
[6] Rabelais (*Prophecies*).
[7] Albrecht Dürer.
[8] Rabelais.

SCENE ONE

The Birth of Gargantua

Gargamelle's Feast begins in an explosion of merriment. In the midst of the company, who are wearing modern dress, Grandgousier and Gargamelle, likewise in modern dress, meet, embrace, and engage in the divine combat. Then they are parted and dressed in their stage costumes. Gargamelle then appears as the picture of motherhood. In one corner of the stage Silenus is sitting on his donkey.

PIERRE AMY, THE PLAY-LEADER (*taking over from the Orator and speaking into a microphone*): Grandgousier was a lusty fellow in his time, who liked his wine heady and his meat salty. Now when he came to the prime of life, he married Gargamelle, daughter of the King of the Butterflies, and a good-looking wench to boot. Well, the pair of them played the two-backed beast together, rubbing their bacon together again, and again, and again, with such good effect that Gargamelle became great with child, a fine son she carried eleven months.

CHORUS OF MEN: A child born of a woman eleven months after her husband's death may be declared legitimate.

CHORUS OF WOMEN: So a widow can safely go buttock-squeezing two months after her husband's dead?

CHORUS OF MEN: If anyone doubts it, a turd for him!

CHORUS: That's right! A turd for him!

GRANDGOUSIER (*in the centre*): Most noble boozers and poxy friends, in celebration of my Gargamelle's condition, I ask you to eat, drink and be merry. Eat every morsel, my lads, to please your bodies and ease your guts! But remember, you bunch of donkey-pricks, to drink my health, and I'll do the same for you.

    Now fill up and drink up and pour it all down!

(The company dance and sing.)

SONG: Let our flagons go ting
    And our goblets all ring
    As we wash the wine down with our laughter.
    All our glasses may weep,
    But we'll drink of them deep,
    And we'll piss it all out not long after.

    Hey nonny, hey nonny, hey nonny no,
    Hither and thither and round we go!

GRANDGOUSIER (*to Gargamelle, who is stuffing herself with tripe*):
    Wife, don't eat so much of that tripe. Your time is near, and
    that's not commendable meat.

GARGAMELLE (*laughing*): Tripe for the tripes, I say! Tripe for the
    tripes!

SONG: You must never go dry
    If you don't want to die,
    So come, lads, and pull out the bung.
    To keep off the thirst,
    I'll always drink first.
    By heavens, that's shitten well sung!

    Hey nonny, hey nonny, hey nonny no,
    Hither and thither and round we go!

[CHORUS OF WOMEN (*to Grandgousier*): In spite of your warnings,
    she's eaten sixteen quarters, two bushels and six pecks of
    tripe!]¹

SONG: When I take the plunge
    I drink like a sponge.
    No bladder holds liquor like mine.
    I bet that you'd lick
    My ugly old prick
    If it pissed the most excellent wine.

---

¹ The passages between square brackets were omitted from the Élysée-
Montmartre production.

Hey nonny, hey nonny, hey nonny no,
Hither and thither and round we go!

A GUEST (*burlesquing the Crucifixion*): I have the word of God on my tongue: *Sitio*.

ANOTHER GUEST: He thirsts!

(*In a parody of the Crucifixion which would be shocking if it were not for the revellers' youth and Joy, Christ is given a drink from a jug of wine, and the spilt liquid is mopped up with a sponge on the end of a spear. Meanwhile*):

A GUEST: For my part, I worship nothing but my belly: the greatest god I know.

CHORUS OF WOMEN: Just look at our Gargamelle, stuffing herself with *godebillios*!

CHORUS OF BOYS: But what are *godebillios*?

CHORUS OF MEN: The fat tripes of *coiros*.

CHORUS OF BOYS: But what are *coiros*?

CHORUS OF MEN: Bullocks fattened in their stalls and on *guimo* meadows.

CHORUS OF BOYS: And what are *guimo* meadows?

CHORUS OF MEN: Meadows that carry two grass crops a year.

(*The Crucifixion group collapses in a roar of merriment.*)

SONG: O *lachryma Christi*!

My eyes are all misty,
My heartbeats are coming much faster.
I know what I'm about,
My apprenticeship's out,
And at drinking I am a Mast Paster.

Hey nonny, hey nonny, hey nonny no,
Hither and thither and round we go!

(*The dancing becomes wilder. The scene resembles a Breughel fair, not so much in its picturesque quality as in the frenzied embraces of the couples.*)

CHORUS OF MEN: Down on the grass with you all!

(*The music and dancing come to a sudden end. Gargamelle begins moaning.*)

CHORUS OF WOMEN: She's beginning to have her pains.

(*They gather round her. Grandgousier goes up to her.*)

GRANDGOUSIER: Be brave, wife: those are the birthpangs you can feel.

Take heart at the coming of your baby.

(*Gargamelle groans.*)

The pain may hurt you, but it won't last long, and the joy that will come after will banish your suffering.

"A woman when she is in travail hath sorrow, because her hour is come, but as soon as she is delivered of the child she remembereth no more the anguish."

(*Gargamelle goes on groaning.*)

Be brave, my sweet ewe. Hurry up with this one, and we'll set about making another.

GARGAMELLE: Oh, it's easy for you men to talk. Still, I'll do my best, since that's what you want. But would to God you had cut it off!

GRANDGOUSIER: Cut what off?

GARGAMELLE: Ha! You're a fine one! You know what I mean.

GRANDGOUSIER: My member? By the goat's blood, if that's what you want, give me a knife!

GARGAMELLE: No, never! God forbid! Don't do anything like that because of what I said. All the same, I'm going to have a lot of trouble today, unless God helps me, and all because of your member and the pleasure it gave you.

GRANDGOUSIER: Be brave, now. You'll be as right as rain. Let the four leading oxen do all the work. I'm away to have another drink. But if you have any trouble, I won't be far off. Just give me a call (*he cups his hands round his mouth*) and I'll come to you right away.

(*Grandgousier walks away. Gargamelle starts writhing in agony.*)

ONE OF THE WOMEN, THEN OTHERS: She's sighing, groaning, screaming.

Ah, here's the child! No, it's her fundament slipping out. That's what comes of eating too much tripe. . . . Look, it's her bum-gut all right.

(*An old woman rushes forward, pushes the bum-gut back, and pours out an astringent for Gargamelle who screams with pain.*)

THE YOUNG WOMAN: The dirty old cow has given her such a horrible potion that her muscles have all closed up. It's an awful thought, but you couldn't even open them with your teeth!

(*The actors rapidly draw a human body on a translucent screen.*[1] *An actor seen in silhouette mimes the foetus trying to get out. All the others gather in front of the screen with their backs to the audience, like a crowd watching a tennis match.*)

ALL: The placenta's working loose! The child is jumping out of the womb and into the hollow vein! It's going up through the diaphragm and past the shoulders! Now it's turning left! Why, look! The little rascal's coming out through the left ear!

(*A huge mask suddenly emerges from the left-hand side of the screen, and the whole theatre is filled with the sound of Gargantua's voice.*)

GARGANTUA: Drink! Drink!

(*An explosion of frantic joy, like that of the crowd at an international match when a goal is scored.*)

GRANDGOUSIER: Garrgh! Aren't you a thirsty one!

ALL (*repeating Grandgousier's words in a gradual crescendo*): Garrgh, aren't you a! Garrg-arn-tua! Gargantua! Gargantua!

(*They gather round the "baby" and play with the huge mask. There is the sound of clinking pint-pots and flagons. Music.*)

GRANDGOUSIER: Pour some drink down his gullet! That should quieten him!

A GIRL: The mere sound of pint-pots and flagons sends him into an ecstasy, as if he were tasting the joys of paradise!

(*The music grows wilder, accompanied by the sound of pint-pots and flagons, popping and farting. A procession forms up, led by Silenus on his donkey.*)

ANOTHER GIRL (*a buxom creature*): Look at him! He's nodding his head in time to the music, popping with his mouth and honking with his arse!

SONG: O *lachryma Christi*!
    My eyes are all misty,
    My heartbeats are coming much faster,

---

[1] Avoid using a film projector. It would be preferable for the actors to improvise drawings on more or less transparent screens, or to mime the birth in full view of the audience.

I know what I'm about,
My apprenticeship's out,
And at drinking I am a Mast Paster.

Hey nonny, hey nonny, hey nonny no,
Hither and thither and round we go!
(*Led by Silenus, the company leave with Gargamelle and "baby" Gargantua, to the sound of frenzied music.*[1] *The music stops.*)

PIERRE AMY, THE PLAY-LEADER (*to the audience*): I rather doubt whether you believe in this strange nativity. If you don't believe in it, I don't care; but a right-minded man, a man of good sense, always believes what he is told.

SCENE TWO
Break the bone
and suck the marrow

THUBAL HOLOFERNES (*representing the spirit of scholasticism, sitting on a throne down right*): Pierre Amy, *mon ami*, that's nothing but foolery and nonsense and childish fantasy.

GRANDGOUSIER (*interrupting him*): Like that fellow Silenus, eh? But you mustn't judge him by his looks, because he's like those boxes you see in apothecaries' shops. They're painted on top with comical figures—harpies, satyrs, bridled geese, horned hares and flying goats—but in olden days they

---

[1] From the very beginning, and especially since Gargamelle's Feast, the mood has been one of immense vitality, childlike exuberance, dionysiac intoxication. "This burlesque prologue introduces us to the book, just as the farces and feasts of the Donkey used to precede the commemoration of the Nativity" (Michelet).

contained rare drugs, balm, ambergris, musk and civet, jewels and other precious things.

Socrates was like that too. Seeing him from the outside, you wouldn't have given an onion-skin for him. But if you'd opened that box, you'd have found a priceless, heavenly drug inside: superhuman understanding, marvellous virtue, invincible courage. (*He recites as if quoting from a poem.*) "The drug within is far more precious than the box doth promise."

THUBAL HOLOFERNES: My dear man, you don't convince me.

PLAY-LEADER: Watch a dog that has found a marrow bone. See how devotedly he eyes it, how carefully he guards it, how fervently he holds it, how cautiously he gnaws it, how diligently he sucks it. What makes him behave like that? What can he hope for in the end? Nothing but a little marrow. Though it's true that a little marrow is tastier than a lot of anything else. (*He recites as if quoting from a poem.*) "Break the bone and suck the substantific marrow!"

GRANDGOUSIER (*who has put on a suit of armour*): Sweet governesses, look after my poppet while I go to conquer the Duchy of Milan. And dress him in white and blue. For white signifies gladness, pleasure, delight and rejoicing. And blue signifies heavenly things.

THUBAL HOLOFERNES (*still grumpy*): White signifies faith, and blue constancy.

(*Fanfare of trumpets. Grandgousier leaves.*)

SCENE THREE

Gargantua the Child

THUBAL HOLOFERNES (*continuing*): And how does young Gargantua spend his time?

A WOMAN (*who may be Gargamelle*): Like the other little children in these parts—eating, drinking and sleeping; drinking, sleeping and eating; sleeping, eating and drinking.

A YOUNG MAN (*sitting in the centre, and speaking as if he were reciting a modern poem*): He was always wallowing in the mud, dirtying his nose, scratching his face and scuffing his shoes. He often gaped at flies and ran after the butterflies who were his father's subjects. He pissed in his shoes, shat in his shirt, wiped his nose on his sleeves, dropped his snot in his soup, and paddled about everywhere. He put the cart before the horse, burnt the candle at both ends, killed two birds with one stone, had his cake and ate it, made a mountain of a molehill, fell between two stools, looked a gift horse in the mouth, struck while the iron was hot, made a virtue of necessity, gathered a rod for his own back, ran with the hare and hunted with the hounds, and lived to fight another day. (*He kneels down and pretends to be stroking three dogs.*) His father's dogs ate out of his dish, and he ate with them. He bit their ears, and they scratched his nose; he blew up their arses, and they licked his lips. (*Three girls gather round the young man and raise him to his feet. A country tune is played on an oboe or flute (?).*)[1] He was always feeling his governesses, upside down, back-to-front, and arse-over-tits. And he had already begun exercising his codpiece, which his governesses decorated every day with nosegays and ribbons and flowers and feathers. (*The three girls begin decorating his codpiece.*)

FIRST GIRL: My bodkin, my ninepin, my coral-branch. . . .

SECOND GIRL: My stopper, my cork, my bung, my spindle, my piercer, my borer, my pillicock, my dingle-dangle.

THIRD GIRL: My battering-ram, my belly-hammer.

SECOND GIRL: My drumstick, my little red sausage, my cocky-wocky.

FIRST GIRL: It's mine. . . .

SECOND GIRL: It belongs to me. . . .

THIRD GIRL: Don't I get any of it? I'll cut it off then, I swear I will.

[1] A question mark in brackets means: optional.

35

FIRST GIRL: Cut it off? Why you'd hurt him! Do you really go around cutting off children's thingummies? Why, if you did that to him, that would be the end of his tail. (*They finish decorating his codpiece and stand back to admire the effect.*)

SCENE FOUR
The Arse-wiper[1]

A fanfare of trumpets.
Grandgousier returns.

GRANDGOUSIER: Well, those Milanese Ganarians have had a real thrashing! And what a joy it is for such a father to come home to such a son! Now we are five, and soon we'll be six. (*To a servant girl.*) Have you kept him sweet and clean? (*Gargantua has been dressed. The part is played by the same actor, in a gay, ingenuous style.*)

SERVANT GIRL: There's no cleaner boy in all the land.

GRANDGOUSIER: How's that?

YOUNG GARGANTUA: Because after long and interesting experiments I've found a method of wiping my arse which is the most lordly, most excellent and most convenient ever known.

GRANDGOUSIER: And what's that?

YOUNG GARGANTUA: I will tell you in a moment. Once I wiped myself with a lady's velvet comforter, and found it good, for the softness of the silk gave a thrill to my fundament.

Another time, I did it with her hood, and that was good too. Then I used her crimson satin ear muffs, but a lot of turdy golden spangles on them took all the skin off my bottom.

---

[1] In spite of its scatological nature, this scene should have a certain 'poetic' charm.

ALL: Oh!

[YOUNG GARGANTUA (*smoothly*): I cured that trouble by wiping myself with a page's bonnet.

ALL: Ah!

YOUNG GARGANTUA: Then, shitting behind a bush, I found a March cat and wiped my arse with it. But its claws scratched the whole of my perineum.

ALL: Ooh!]

YOUNG GARGANTUA (*smoothly*): I healed myself of that next day by wiping myself with my mother's gloves, which were perfumed with benjamin.

ALL: Ah!

(*Music (?).*)

YOUNG GARGANTUA (*swaying about voluptuously*): Then I wiped myself with sage, fennel, dill, marjoram, roses, gourd leaves, cabbages, blites, vine-shoots, marsh-mallows, mullein, lettuces, spinach-leaves, persicaria, nettles and comfrey.

But these things gave me the Lombardy flux, from which I was cured by wiping myself with my codpiece.

(*Music stops.*)

GRANDGOUSIER: Yes, but which arse-wiper did you find the best?

YOUNG GARGANTUA: I was coming to that, and soon you'll know too.

(*Music (?).*)

I wiped myself with the curtains, a cushion, a carpet, a napkin, a handkerchief and a wrapper; with hay, straw, rushes, flock, wool and paper. But (*recited*):
Who his foul arse with paper wipes
Leaves chips behind from out his tripes.

(*Music stops.*)

GRANDGOUSIER: What, you little rascal, have you been at the pot, that you can rhyme already?

YOUNG GARGANTUA: Yes, Your Majesty, I can rhyme that much and more, and sometimes I rhyme until I get the rheum! (*Cries of admiration.*) [Do you want me to go on?

GRANDGOUSIER: Yes, indeed.

YOUNG GARGANTUA: But will you buy me a puncheon of Breton wine if I know more than you on the subject?]

GRANDGOUSIER: Oh, what a clever young fellow you are! One of these days I'll have you made a Doctor of Merry Learning, by God, for you've more wit than years. Now carry on with your arse-wiping discourse [and, by my beard, you shall have sixty pipes of that good Breton wine which doesn't grow in Brittany, but in the good land of Verron.][1]

YOUNG GARGANTUA: Next I wiped myself with a kerchief, a pillow, a slipper, a game-bag and a hat. And mark you, some hats are smooth and others shaggy, some are velvet and others satin. The best of all, to my mind, are the shaggy ones.

Then I wiped myself with a hen, a cock, a calf's skin, a hare, a pigeon and a cormorant.

But in conclusion I say and maintain that there's no arse-wiper to compare with a downy goose, provided you hold her neck between your legs. You can take my word for it, you really can. You get a marvellous feeling in your arse-hole, both from the softness of the down and the warmth of the goose, which is easily communicated to the bum-gut and other intestines, even reaching the heart and the brain.

(*Sighs of pleasure and cries of admiration from all.*)

GRANDGOUSIER: By my faith, from what I have just heard I can tell that my son's understanding springs from some divine source, he is so acute, subtle, profound and serene. If he is well taught he will attain a supreme degree of wisdom. (*He turns towards Master Holofernes.*)

[1] Muscadet.

Medieval Education[1]

GRANDGOUSIER (*continuing*): Master Thubal Holofernes, great
doctor and sophist that you are, what sort of education do
you advise for my son? (*A young actor, preferably the actor
playing Young Gargantua, performs a mime to match the text,
looking increasingly stupid.*)

HOLOFERNES: The learned education of our medieval schools.
Five years and three months to learn the alphabet well
enough to say it backwards. Thirteen years, six months and
two weeks for Donat, Facet, Theodolet, Latin grammar,
common civility and learning the Gothic script to copy out
his books.

GRANDGOUSIER: What! You mean to say the art of printing isn't
practised yet?

HOLOFERNES: What heresy! You'll be suggesting he learns Greek
next!

In accordance with the rules of our schools, he will get up
between eight and nine, [for "it is vain to rise before the
sun". (*Recites.*)

"Wherefore be an early riser?
Early drinking is much wiser."
(*Grotesque church music (?).*)

Then he will] go to church and hear anything from
twenty-six to thirty Masses. He will mumble all sorts of
litanies, fingering them so carefully that not a single grain
falls to the ground. Then, walking up and down the cloisters,
he will say more rosaries than sixteen hermits.
(*Music stops.*)

[1] This scene should be grotesque and almost repulsive.

And when his mind turns to the kitchen, he will drink an enormous draught of white wine to relieve his kidneys.

For the only limit to drinking should be when the drinker finds his cork soles swelling six inches.

Look at that young lord. He's studying well and giving all his time to his lessons. (*The "young lord" now looks like the complete village idiot.*)

GRANDGOUSIER: But he's making no progress, and what's worse, he looks silly, simple-minded, dreamy and doltish. It would be better for him to learn nothing at all.

PONOCRATES, THE HUMANIST (*sitting on a throne down left*): How is it that in the bright light of our times there are still men here and there who will not raise their eyes from the thick fog of Gothic barbarism towards the glorious radiance of the sun?

GRANDGOUSIER: Ponocrates, how is a young man brought up in France nowadays?

PONOCRATES: Not in this vicious Gothic manner. But we must treat your son tolerantly at first, for Nature cannot bear sudden changes without great violence.

Eudemon, show us, while I explain.

SCENE SIX

Humanist Education[1]

A very handsome young man appears, between eighteen and twenty years old. He performs a mime, not illustrating the text, but in counterpoint to it.

PONOCRATES: In France a young man rises about four in the morning.

[1] In contrast to the grotesque character of medieval education, this scene should give an impression of great purity and beauty.

While he is being rubbed down, a chapter of Holy Writ is read to him loudly and clearly, showing God's majesty and wondrous wisdom.

Once he is dressed, combed and perfumed, he goes out into the meadows and plays ball or tennis, exercising his body as he has already exercised his mind.

All these sports are a form of freedom.

At table, when Master Appetite calls, he converses joyfully about bread, wine, water, salt, meat, fish, fruit, herbs and roots, shrubs and bushes, all the plants in the earth and all the metals hidden in the abysses.

He masters other languages: Greek, Latin, Hebrew, Chaldean, Arabic.

He pores over Plato and Cicero.

He studies medicine until no physician knows half as much as he.

He examines ancient texts and explores the liberal arts: sciences, mathematics, geometry, astronomy, music.

(*Renaissance music* (*Goudimel?*).)

He sings with others in four or five parts, on a given theme, to their throats' content. He learns to play the lute, the spinet, the harp, the flute, the viol and the sackbut.

Leaving his lodgings with a riding-master, he learns the art of horsemanship.

(*Drums.*)

He mounts a charger, a cob, a jennet, a barb, clearing ditches, jumping fences, turning short.

He breaks a lance, brandishes a pike, wields a two-handed sword.

He hunts the stag, the bear, the boar, the hare, the partridge, the pheasant and the bustard.

He wrestles, runs, jumps and swims. He swims in deep water, on his belly, on his back, on his side, with just his feet, or with an overarm motion. He dives headfirst into the water, exploring the rocks, sounding the depths.

He climbs trees like a cat, and leaps from one to another like a squirrel.

And to strengthen his sinews, he exercises with two great

sows of lead, which are known as dumb-bells.
(*The lighting changes to suggest night. Soft music.*)

At night we gaze upon the face of the sky, noting any
comets and the situations, aspects, oppositions and conjunctions of the stars.
(*Organ music.*)

Then, praying to God the Creator, and reaffirming our
faith in Him, we glorify Him for His immense goodness,
(*Hymns.*)
thanking Him for the past and commending ourselves to His
divine clemency for the future.
(*Music stops.*)

[However, once a month, our young men spend the whole
day making merry:
(*Frenzied music (rock and roll?).*)
joking, frolicking, drinking, playing, singing, dancing,
romping in some fair meadow, unnesting sparrows, taking
quails, and fishing for frogs and crayfish.
(*Dancing.*)

SONGS:
1. O God of kindness, God of might,
   Who once turned water into wine,
   Change my bum to a lantern-light
   To give my neighbour arsehole-shine.
2. She saw her husband fully armed,
   Save for his codpiece, going to fight,
   And said: "My dear, in case you're harmed,
   Arm that, which is my chief delight."
   For these words does she merit blame?
   I say no, thinking of her fear
   That things would never be the same
   Without the piece she held so dear.

(*Dancing stops, and the mood changes back to refined elegance.*)[1]

PONOCRATES (*continuing*): Sometimes we seek the company of
scholars, or of men who have visited foreign lands. And
sitting in the laurel groves, we recite by heart verses from

[1] This brief orgiastic interlude should offer a striking contrast to the rest
of the scene.

42

Hesiod and Virgil, write witty epigrams in Latin, and turn them into French. For it is right and proper that we should speak the language of our country as others speak it.]

EUDEMON: O Erasmus, kindly father,
    What I am
    And what I do
    I owe to you alone.

(*Darkness gradually falls. During this time, the actors have taken their places for the Picrocholine War. A portrait of Rabelais is lit up, while the recorded voice of the Orator is heard.*)

ORATOR'S VOICE: At Ligugé, this September
    Sixth, I beg you to remember,
    Resting in my bed this day,
    Your friend and servant, Rabelais.

(*Renaissance music ends. Lighting changes. Recorded echo.*)
    At Ligugé, this September
    Sixth. . . .

SCENE SEVEN

Picrochole[1]

A. The Sweet Life: The Incident

1st Setting: The Fireside at La Devinière

GRANDGOUSIER: In the first days of September the wine harvest begins. . . .

2nd Setting: Centre-Stage

PLAY-LEADER: The shepherds of these parts are busy guarding the vines to prevent the starlings from eating the grapes.

---

[1] *Picrochole* is the longest *divertissement* in the whole of *Rabelais*. It combines a circus atmosphere with the style of Alfred Jarry's *Ubu Roi*. The actors should play this scene like circus clowns.

(*Mime by the Shepherds.*)

At the same time the farmers nearby are gathering nuts with their long poles.

(*Mime by the Farmers.*)

And the bakers of Lerné are passing by along the road, taking ten or twelve loads of cakes to town.

FROGIER, LEADER OF THE SHEPHERDS (*to the Bakers*): Good neighbours of Lerné, would you be good enough to sell us some of your cakes, for cash, at the market price? For fresh cakes with grapes for breakfast is food fit for the gods!

MARQUET, LEADER OF THE BAKERS: Not to you toothless louts!

A SHEPHERD: Poxy ballbags!

BAKERS, SHEPHERDS, FARMERS (*all together*): Scabs, boors, dunderheads, idiots, rogues, milksops, scoundrels, cheats, good-fornothings, shitten shepherds, bastard bakers! (*They fight.*) Murder! Help! There's one for your coronal joint! There's one for your crotaphic artery!

A FARMER: That's the way—as if you're threshing green rye!

BAKERS (*running away*): You'll be sorry for this! (*Picrochole pops up like a jack-in-the-box.*)

PLAY-LEADER. These little quarrels often lead to big battles. (*Suddenly the rest of the company rush into the theatre, sweeping across it like a noisy political demonstration, waving all sorts of banners, placards and portraits, and bellowing imaginary national anthems. This sort of human tidal wave will reappear like a motif.*)

3rd Setting: The fireside at La Devinière, where Grandgousier and Gargamelle are still enjoying the pleasures of life.

GARGAMELLE: In the meantime my old man, Grandgousier, sits by a nice warm fire after supper, warming his balls. And while his chestnuts are roasting, he writes on the hearth with the charred end of a stick we use for poking the fire. (*Roll of drums.*)

PLAY-LEADER (*holding microphone*): War has broken out! Picrochole, the King of Lerné, has taken the quarrel over the cakes as an excuse to invade the whole country. (*Drums and trumpets in the distance. Picrochole, his General Staff, and his troops all pop up like jack-in-the-boxes.*)

44

SHEPHERD PILLOT (*to Grandgousier*): Help us, Grandgousier! Our neighbours of Lerné have attacked us and are laying waste the whole country, sparing neither rich nor poor, neither church nor cottage.

They are driving away oxen, cows, bulls, calves, heifers, ewes, rams, she-goats, he-goats, hens, capons, chickens, goslings, ganders, geese, hogs, sows and piglets.

They are shaking down our nuts, stripping our vines, carrying off our vine-stocks, and picking all the fruit on our trees!

GRANDGOUSIER: Alas, my good people, alack, my friends, I wanted nothing in my old age but repose, and all my life I have sought peace above all else. But now I shall have to load my tired, weak shoulders with armour, to help and protect my poor subjects. Justice demands I do that, for I am supported by their labour and fed by their sweat—I, my children, and my family.

B. THE CLOSE AT SEUILLÉ

PILLOT: Now they are at Seuillé. They've encircled the abbey and broken down the walls of the close.

(*The monks gather up-stage, to the accompaniment of tolling bells and grotesque organ music, chanting:* Im, nim, pe, ne, ne, ne, ne, tum, ne, ne, num, num, ini, i, mi, i, mi, o, o, ne, o, o, ne, no, ne, no, num, ne, num, num.[1] *They will go on chanting like this as far as:* "*Slit the throats. . . .*"

Help us, Friar John!

Friar John of the Funnels appears, looking like a Samurai with the staff of his cross in his hands.)

FRIAR JOHN (*to the chanting monks*): By God, that's shitten well sung!

A MONK: How dare you disturb the divine service!

FRIAR JOHN: But what about the wine service? "Farewell baskets, the harvest is in!" (*He advances on the enemy.*) God's belly! That's Church property, so take your hands off it! (*His place in the fight is taken by a wrestler in a cowl—a Franciscan*

[1] This is the text as Rabelais wrote it.

45

cowl—while he gives a commentary into a microphone on the end of his cross. Recorded music in the background.)

He bashed the brains out of some, cracked the arms and legs of others, disjointed the necks of these, and broke the backs of those. He flattened their noses, blackened their eyes, smashed their jaw-bones, knocked their teeth in, shattered their shoulder blades, hammered their hips, shivered their shins, and thumped their thighs.

If anybody tried to hide among the thickest vines, he ran his stick down his spine and broke his back like a dog.

If anybody tried to run away, he smashed his head to smithereens along the lamdoidal join.

PILLOT: And if anybody climbed a tree, thinking he'd be safe up there, he pushed his staff up his fundament.

FRIAR JOHN (*running after a soldier who is trying to get away*): The devil take you, if he will!

(*The recorded background music is accompanied by the following shouts:* Saint Barbara! Saint George! Saint Pancras! Our Lady of Cunault! Our Lady of Loreto! Our Lady of Good News! Our Lady of Lenou! Our Lady of Rivière! Saint James! Saint Cadouyn! Saint John of Angély! Saint Eutropius of Saintes! Saint Mesmes of Chinon! Saint Martin of Candes! Saint Cloud of Cinays! The relics of Javrezay!)

PILLOT: He ran them through the chest, through the mediastinum, through the heart. Or he ran them between the ribs and turned the stomach upside down.

A LITTLE MONKLING: Others he ran through the navel so hard that their bowels gushed out. And others he ran through the balls and up the bum-gut.

PILLOT: Some died without speaking, and others spoke without dying. Some died as they spoke, and others spoke as they died.

(*The dying cry out:* Confession! Confession! Confiteor! Miserere! In manus!)

FRIAR JOHN: Slit the throats of anyone you find on the ground.

(*The chanting stops as the monks join in the slaughter.*)

A MONK (*dragging three straw dummies*): These men have confessed their sins and expressed contrition.

46

FRIAR JOHN: Then they've earned their pardon and they'll go to heaven as straight as a sickle. (*He executes them, and arms, legs and heads fly into the air. A final cry of terror and all the noise dies away.*)

PILLOT (*coming back towards Grandgousier*): Thus, by Friar John's prowess, all those troops who had entered the close were discomfited, to the number of thirteen thousand, six hundred and twenty-two, not counting the women and children.

C. NEGOTIATIONS

PLAY-LEADER (*speaking into his microphone*): Meanwhile Picrochole is advancing. He occupies the Castle of La Roche-Clermaud and entrenches himself there with his men. (*Picrochole's camp with his General Staff, four clowns.*)

GRANDGOUSIER (*to one of his men*): Basque, go and fetch Gargantua post-haste. (*To another.*) As for you, Ulrich Gallet, go to Picrochole and tell him that my purpose is not to provoke but to appease, not to attack but to defend. . . .
(*On Picrochole's side.*)

TOUCHFAUCET (*One of the four staff officers*): Those yokels are scared stiff. Grandgousier is shitting himself for fear, the poor old boozer!

EARLYPEAR: Lick a villain and he'll prick you; prick a villain and he'll lick you.

GALLET (*on the side of Picrochole's camp*): Open the castle gates!

PICROCHOLE: Come and get your cakes yourself! They're soft and bollocky. But I won't open the gates to you.

GALLET (*going back to Grandgousier*): There's no hope of bringing them to terms except by a short, sharp war.

GRANDGOUSIER: Oh, God, my Saviour, help me, inspire me, advise me what to do. And I shall have your Gospel preached clearly, simply and in its entirety.
(*Change of lighting. The actors rush through the theatre again with flags, banners, etc.*)

D. Council of War Under Picrochole

Picrochole looks like Charles V. But he holds the map of the world like Charlie Chaplin in The Great Dictator. *With him are his staff officers.*

TOUCHFAUCET: Sire, today we are going to make you the happiest and most chivalrous prince that ever was since Alexander of Macedonia.

PICROCHOLE: You may put on your hats.

DUNGHILL: Thank you, sire. Our plan is that you will leave a captain garrisoned here with a small company of men, to hold the place, which seems strong enough to us, both by its nature and by its ramparts. You will then divide your army in two parts.

TOUCHFAUCET: One part will fall upon this fellow Grandgousier and his men, and will easily rout him at the first attack. That victory will fill your coffers, because no noble prince ever has a penny. Hoarding money is the mark of a villain.

EARLYPEAR: In the meantime the other part of your army will make for Aunis, Saintonge, Angoumois and Gascony, pressing on to Périgord, Médoc and the Landes. Cities, castles and fortresses will fall to you without a fight. At Bayonne, Saint-Jean-de-Luz and Fuenterrabia you will seize all the shipping; and sailing along the coast towards Galicia and Portugal, you will pillage every port as far as Lisbon, where you will find all the supplies a conqueror requires. Spain will surrender, by God, for the Spaniards are a race of simpletons.

PICROCHOLE: Yokels!

EARLYPEAR: Going through the Straits of Gibraltar, you will erect two pillars there greater than the Pillars of Hercules, as a perpetual memorial to your name, and the straits shall be called the Picrocholine Sea.

When you have passed through the Picrocholine Sea, Barbarossa will surrender to you. . . .

PICROCHOLE: I shall grant him his life.

TOUCHFAUCET: Certainly, provided he agrees to be baptized, he and the Jews he has saved. Then you will attack the kingdoms of Tunis, Bizerta, Algeria, Bône, Cyrene, and indeed the whole of Barbary. Pressing onwards, you will lay your hands on Majorca, Minorca, Sardinia, Corsica and the Balearics. You will subdue Genoa, Florence and Lucca, and you'll make short work of Rome. Poor Master Pope is already half-dead with fright.

PICROCHOLE: I'll never kiss his slipper, I can tell you that.

DUNGHILL: Once Italy is taken, Naples, Calabria, Apulia and Sicily will be sacked, and Malta too. I only hope those funny knights of theirs resist you, so that we can see the colour of their urine!

PICROCHOLE: I'd like to go to Loreto.

TOUCHFAUCET: No, no! You can do that on your way home. From Malta we shall take Crete, Cyprus, Rhodes and the Cyclades, and fall upon Morea. Once that is ours, then by Saint Trinian, God preserve Jerusalem! For all the Sultan's power is nothing compared to yours!

PICROCHOLE: Then I'll rebuild Solomon's temple.

TOUCHFAUCET: Not yet. Wait a little. You mustn't be in such a hurry. Do you know what Octavian Augustus said? "Make haste slowly." First it would be best for you to conquer Asia Minor as far as the Euphrates.

PICROCHOLE: Shall we see Babylon and Mount Sinai?

EARLYPEAR: There'll be no need for that! Isn't it enough to have crossed the Caspian Sea and ridden through both Armenias and all three Arabias?

(*Military tunes of all countries and all times, especially modern times.*)

PICROCHOLE (*stopping playing with the map of the world*): Why, we must be mad! Fools that we are!

ALL (*in astonishment*): Why, what's the matter?

PICROCHOLE: What are we going to drink in those deserts? They say Julian Augustus and his army died of thirst out there.

EARLYPEAR: We've already seen to all that. In the Syrian Sea you have nine thousand and fourteen great ships laden with the best wines in the world. They put in at Jaffa, where there are twenty-two hundred thousand camels and sixteen hundred elephants which you took in a single hunt when you entered Libya. There's also the whole of the Mecca

49

caravan. Won't they provide you with enough wine?

PICROCHOLE: I suppose so, but it won't be fresh.

TOUCHFAUCET: Ye gods and little fishes! A great warrior and conqueror who wants to rule the world can't always have everything to his liking.

PICROCHOLE: But while all this is going on, what is the other part of the army doing that defeated that boozer Grandgousier?

DUNGHILL: They aren't being idle. They have taken Brittany for you, and Normandy, Flanders, Hainault, Brabant, Artois, Holland and Zealand. They have crossed the Rhine over the bellies of the Swiss, and some of them have subdued Luxemburg, Lorraine, Champagne and Savoy as far as Lyons, where they have found your forces returning from their naval victories in the Mediterranean. They have reassembled in Bohemia, after plundering Swabia, Württemburg, Bavaria, Austria, Moravia and Styria. Then they have fallen upon Lübeck, Norway, Sweden, Denmark and Gothland. From there, sailing across the sandy Baltic and Sarmatia, they have conquered Prussia, Poland, Lithuania, Russia, Wallachia, Transylvania, Hungary, Bulgaria and Turkey, and are now at Constantinople.

PICROCHOLE: Then let's join up with them as soon as possible, for I want to be Emperor of Trebizond as well.

ECHEPHRON, A WISE OLD MAN:[1] I very much fear that all these adventures will come to nothing. What do you want with all these conquests? What will be the result of all this fighting and travelling?

PICROCHOLE: The result will be that when we return we shall rest in comfort.

ECHEPHRON: But in case you shouldn't return, for it's a long and dangerous journey, wouldn't it be better for us to rest now and not expose ourselves to all those risks?

EARLYPEAR: By God, what an old dodderer! Let's go and hide in the inglenook, and spend our lives threading beads with the ladies.

Nothing venture, nothing gain.

ECHEPHRON: Nothing venture, nothing lose.

[1] This part may be spoken by Ponocrates.

PICROCHOLE (*in a fit of hysteria*): That's enough! Let's go! I
bite, charge, strike, catch and kill! On! On! Make haste!
And let him who loves me follow me!
(*Great fanfare of trumpets. Darkness falls over the Picrochole
camp.*)

E. GARGANTUA'S RETURN[1]

PLAY-LEADER (*speaking into microphone*): Gargantua, riding his
great mare, has just crossed the Nun's Bridge near La
Roche-Clermaud. He's found a huge tall tree on his way
here, and pulled it out of the ground, and stripped off the
branches to use it as a staff and a spear. Now he's crossing
the wood of Vede and arriving outside the castle.

GARGANTUA'S VOICE (*recorded*): Are you there, or are you not?
If you are, be off with you. If you aren't, I've nothing to say.
(*A cannon shot.*)

PLAY-LEADER: A cannon-ball has hit him on the temple!

GARGANTUA'S VOICE (*recorded*): Are you throwing grape pips at
me? That vintage will cost you dear!
(*A tremendous cannonade.*)

PLAY-LEADER: From the towers and battlements they're firing
over nine thousand and twenty-five falconet and arquebus
shots at his head.

GARGANTUA'S VOICE (*recorded*): These flies are blinding me. Give
me a branch from those willows to drive them off.

PLAY-LEADER: Now he's striking the castle with his great tree,
smashing the towers and battlements, and reducing everything to ruins.

Now he's come to a garden and asked if there are any
lettuces there to make a salad. He's pulled up as many as he
fancies, and with them half a dozen pilgrims who were
hiding between the cabbages and peas.

And he's swallowed all six of them.

PONOCRATES: Even a king must eat!

[1] A huge balloon effigy of Gargantua, over 15 feet high, will be used for
this scene.

F. GRANDGOUSIER'S BANQUET

Grandgousier is holding a victory banquet. Fanfares of trumpets. Friar John enters with Touchfaucet as his prisoner. The banquet begins. Harp music in the background.

GRANDGOUSIER: Ha! Friar John, my friend, Friar John, my cousin, Friar John, by all the devils, let me give you a hug!

GYMNAST, GARGANTUA'S SQUIRE: You old ball-bag, let me squeeze you till I break your back.

FRIAR JOHN: It was nothing really. I can't sleep at night if I haven't done a brave deed during the day.

GRANDGOUSIER: Come, come, take a stool beside me, at this end.

(Basque serves each in turn.)

FRIAR JOHN: Boy, pour me some wine so that I can have a gargle. Then I'll drink to you, by God, and to your horse, with all my heart.

I'll eat well too: my stomach's always gaping open like a lawyer's purse.

Page, pour away! Ah, that's better! How good God is to give us this good wine!

I swear to God, if I'd lived in the time of Jesus Christ, I'd have hamstrung those Apostles who ran away like cowards after a good supper and left their master in the lurch.

I hate a man worse than poison who runs away when he ought to be using his knife.

Oh, if only I could be King of France for eighty or a hundred years! By God, I'd cut the balls off those dogs who fled from Pavia!

Isn't it better and more honourable to die fighting bravely than to live running shamefully?

PONOCRATES: Friar John, you know what the French are like: they are good for nothing except at the first attack. Then they are fiercer than devils, but if they delay they are worse than women!

(They drink.)

FRIAR JOHN: By the Pope's holy balls! Now tell me, what sort of wine did you drink in Paris?

And why the devil did you have to go studying?

Now *I* don't study—never have. In our abbey we never study for fear of the mumps. Our late Abbot used to say a learned monk was a monstrous thing. And he was right, by God!

PONOCRATES: What, do you swear, Friar John?

FRIAR JOHN: It's to embellish my language. To give it a little colour, a little Ciceronian rhetoric.

PONOCRATES: By my faith as a Christian, this is an entertaining monk! So why do people call monks spoil-sports and exclude them from all good company?

GRANDGOUSIER: The reason is that they eat the shit of the world —I mean our sins—and as shiteaters they are very properly banished to their privies, the convents and monasteries, and cut off from polite society.

If you can understand why a pet monkey in a house is always teased and tormented by the family, you will understand why monks are shunned by all, young and old alike. The monkey doesn't guard the house like a dog; it doesn't pull the plough like an ox; it doesn't produce milk or wool like a cow or a sheep; and it doesn't carry burdens like a horse.

Similarly a monk doesn't till the fields like a peasant, doesn't guard the country like a soldier, doesn't cure the sick like a doctor, doesn't preach and teach like a good evangelist [and pedagogue, and doesn't carry goods and provisions like a merchant].

That is the reason why everyone spurns and abhors them.

GYMNAST: Yes, but they pray to God for us.

PONOCRATES: Nothing of the sort. It's true that they annoy the whole neighbourhood with their jangling bells. And they mumble lots of legends and psalms and Our Fathers and Hail Marys, without understanding them or thinking about them. That's what I call mocking God, not praying to Him.

GARGANTUA'S VOICE (*recorded*): But good Friar John is no bigot. He works and toils; he defends the oppressed; he comforts the afflicted; he helps the needy; and he guards the close of his abbey.

GYMNAST: Why, yes, comrades, the war isn't over yet, and our

53

enemies are ten times as many as we are. Shall we charge them?

FRIAR JOHN: Do you judge men by their numbers, and not by their valour and courage? Of course we must charge them!

GRANDGOUSIER: We must do nothing of the kind. For according to the art of war you must never drive your enemy to desperate straits. Such a plight multiplies his strength and increases his courage. How many victories have the vanquished wrested from their conquerors' hands, when the victors, against all reason, have tried to wipe out their enemy completely, without leaving a single man alive to bear the news! Always leave every door and every road open to your enemies, and build them a bridge of silver to help them run away.

Come here, Touchfaucet. . . .

PONOCRATES: How happy the world would be if kings were philosophers and philosophers were kings!

GRANDGOUSIER: Touchfaucet, tell us about Picrochole's plans and the state of his affairs.

TOUCHFAUCET: Milord, his aim and purpose is to conquer the whole country, if he can, to avenge the insult to his bakers.

GRANDGOUSIER: The time is past for the conquering of kingdoms to the detriment of our Christian brothers and neighbours. [This imitation of the Herculeses, Alexanders, Hannibals, Scipios and Caesars of old is contrary to the teaching of the Gospel, which commands each of us to guard, protect, rule and administer his own lands, and not to invade those of others.] What the Saracens and Barbarians formerly called deeds of prowess, we now call robbery and wickedness.

Go your way, Touchfaucet, in God's name, and show your king the error of his ways. I shall have your arms and horse returned to you.

Here is a Vienne sword with a scabbard of chased gold, and a gold collar set with precious stones.[1]

This is how neighbours and old friends should behave to one another.

(*Touchfaucet returns to Picrochole's camp.*)

[1] Touchfaucet reels under the weight of the collar.

For our part, since Picrochole won't listen to reason, let us take counsel.

PILLOT: Picrochole has fled. Picrochole has disappeared.

PONOCRATES: Thus do all conquerers end.

GRANDGOUSIER (*centre-stage*): I am sorry that he has gone, for I would have given him to understand that this war was waged against my will, and without any hope of increasing my fame or possessions. But since he has vanished, and nobody knows what has become of him, it is my desire that his kingdom shall pass in its entirety to his son. He is now only five years old, but he shall never be a hostage.[1]

To each of you I give in perpetuity—unless he dies without heirs—my castles and adjoining lands. To Ponocrates, La Roche-Clermaud; to Gymnast, Le Coudray; to Eudemon, Montpensier; to Ithybole, Montsoreau; Gravot to Sebaste; and Quinquenay to Alexander....

FRIAR JOHN: You are the finest fellow who ever buckled on a sword.

PONOCRATES: You take everything in good part; you put the best construction on every deed; and you are never troubled or shocked.

GRANDGOUSIER: That is because nothing on earth and under heaven is worthy to stir our emotions or trouble our minds.

But I still have this monk to provide for. Friar John, I make you Abbot of Seuillé.

FRIAR JOHN: I cannot accept, Milord. For how could I govern others when I can't govern myself?

But if it seems to you that I have done you a service, and may do you more in the future, give me leave to found an abbey after my own heart, with a religious order contrary to all others.

GRANDGOUSIER: Your request pleases me, and I offer you the entire district of Thelema, beside the River Loire. Now tell us of your new religious order.

(*Friar John sweeps everyone away with a broad gesture. Corresponding chord of music.*)

---

[1] As were the children of François I, notably the future Henri II, in Spain.

SCENE EIGHT

The Abbey of Thelema[1]

FRIAR JOHN: First of all, there shall be no walls around my abbey. For all other abbeys have high walls around them, and the monks become quite wall-eyed.

Because everything in this world is encompassed, limited and regulated by hours, there shall be no clocks or sundials here. For the greatest waste of time I know is to count the hours.

ORATOR: The hours are made for man and not man for the hours.

(*All sorts of ugly creatures enter in readiness for the mime.*)

FRIAR JOHN: Because no women are put into nunneries unless they are one-eyed, lame, hunchbacked, ugly, deformed, mad, half-witted, cursed or diseased—for what can you do with a woman who is neither good nor pretty?

PLAY-LEADER: Send her to a nunnery.

ORATOR: Or make a sempstress of her.

FRIAR JOHN: No women shall be admitted unless they are beautiful, well-developed and sweet-natured.

(*The ugly women become beauties. They are joined by the men.*[2])

Because in the religious houses women are kept apart from men, except when they meet in secrecy and stealth, here there shall be no women without men and no men without women.

Because both men and women, once accepted into a

[1] This scene should not be allowed to fall into the trap of ballet. The dramatic game' must be predominant, though heightened by singing and dancing. There should be no superfluous gestures.

[2] The men and women, of our time or Rabelais's, blend naturally together. The long hair of the period or of today's hippies, bare breasts after the Clouet fashion, miniskirts, etc.

religious order, are forced and compelled to remain in it all their lives, here both men and women, once accepted, shall be able to leave whenever they wish, without let or hindrance.

Because monks and nuns generally make three vows—of chastity, poverty and obedience—here it shall be ordained that anyone can be married, that anyone can be rich, and that everyone can live in liberty.

(*Mime and dance.*)

CHORALE: Enter not here, you hypocrites and bigots,
      Sacristy beetles with noses like spigots.

(*The bigots are rejected.*)

      Enter not here, you lawyers and judges
      Who make your money from quarrels and grudges.

(*The judges and doctors of the Sorbonne are rejected. Entry of the Humanists and Reformers, led by Abelard.*)

      Enter in here, you who nurture and preach,
      Who clearly and simply God's teaching expound,
      To vanquish His foes by writing and speech
      And make this a home of Religion Profound.

(*Entry of the Knights, led by François I.*)

      Enter in here, all you nobles and knights.
      Merry and cheerful and handsome and gay.
      Here you'll receive all your chivalrous rights
      And find entertainment and joy every day.

FRIAR JOHN: And everything shall be done as the ladies wish it.

(*Entry of the women, led by Marguerite of Navarre.*)

CHORALE: Enter in here, all you ladies of birth,
      Fear not to spend as you will of our treasure.
      Flowers of beauty, exemplars of mirth,
      Join us in tasting the sweet life of pleasure.

(*The mime turns into a tennis game, with the sun as the ball.*)

FRIAR JOHN: We shall get up when we wish, and eat, drink, work and sleep when the fancy takes us.

(*A blaze of light. Everyone dances, led by François I, Marguerite of Navarre and Abelard.*)

ALL: The sun! The sun!
    Do as you will

Because people are free!
(*The music and dancing rise to a frenzied pitch followed by a strange torpor.*)

SCENE NINE

The Birth of Pantagruel[1]

MODERN ORATOR: Alas, freedom didn't last for long. After the victory of Marignano came the defeat of Pavia! Treachery and captivity!

FRANÇOIS I: I was defeated and a prisoner made,
        And taken round the camp, a captive king,
        Here and there to all the foe displayed.

ORATOR: The great liberal, humanist movement in Europe was broken.

PLAY-LEADER: These were hard times for France. Marguerite of Navarre, the Marguerite of Marguerites, cried her heart out. And in his dungeon in Madrid, our headstrong, handsome king, who could have advised not only artists but also gardeners and farmers, thought sadly of all those who trusted him.

FRANÇOIS I (*looking through the rungs of a ladder*):
        Nymphs, when shall I see again
        The waters of the Loire and Seine,
        The Rhône, the Rhine, the Pyrenees?
        Where is the king you did so please?

[1] Just as the spirit of *Gargantua* was the spirit of Marignano, a spirit of victory, exuberance and youth, of pure Joy, of superabundant life, so the spirit of *Pantagruel* is the spirit of Pavia, in other words the spirit of defeat, suffering and misery. This should make a poignant contrast. Something has been broken. And the fact is, if there had been no Pavia, a humanist Europe might have been created and there might have been no wars of religion.

ORATOR: These were years of drought and taxes, intrigue and poverty.

CHORUS: Years of horror!

(*All the actors are sad, silent, preoccupied.*)

[ORATOR (*thoughtfully*): Gargantua was born in joy and exuberance, and his mother's womb was itself gigantic. If Pantagruel was born a giant, it was in reaction to the sadness of the times, and his mother Badebec died giving birth to him.]

ONE OF THE ACTORS (*trying to revive the company's spirits*): Gargantua, at the age of four hundred, four score and forty-four years, begat his son Pantagruel by his wife Badebec, daughter of the King of the Amaurots in Utopia, who died in childbirth; for he was so wondrous large and heavy that he could not come into the world without killing his mother.

In order to understand fully the cause and reason of that name which was given to him at baptism, you must know that in that year there was so great a drought throughout the land of Africa that thirty-six months, three weeks, four days, thirteen hours and a few minutes went by without rain, and with such fierce heat that the whole earth was parched.

ANOTHER ACTOR: There was not a single tree on earth that had either leaf or flower; the grass was withered, the rivers drained, the springs all dry; the poor fish writhing and shrieking on the ground; the birds falling from the air for want of dew. Wolves, foxes, stags, boars, deer, hares, weasels, martens, badgers and other animals were found dead in the fields, their mouths agape. As for men, they were in a pitiful state. You could see them with their tongues hanging out like greyhounds. Some jumped into wells, and others entered cows' bellies to be in the shade.

PLAY-LEADER: The whole country was in the doldrums.

(*The actors are huddled in corners. Silence.*)

FIRST ACTOR: It was then that Pantagruel was born. And that was why his father gave him the name he did: for *Panta* in Greek means *all*, and *Gruel* in the Hagarene language means *thirsty*, signifying that at the time of his birth the world was all parched. [He also saw in a vision that one day his son would rule over the thirsty.

SOMEBODY (*in a sort of trance*): The Pantagruel has got me by the throat! A drink! A drink!]

SECOND ACTOR: When Pantagruel was born, nobody could have been more astounded and perplexed than his father Gargantua; for seeing on the one hand his wife Badebec dead, and on the other hand his son Pantagruel born, and wondrous big and handsome, he did not know what to say or do.

GARGANTUA (*now played by an old actor of normal height*): Shall I weep or shan't I? Why, yes, because my good wife is dead, who was the most this and the most that in the whole world. To live without her is just to waste away. Ah, Badebec, my darling, my sweetheart, my little cunt—though in fact it measured a good three acres and two roods—my poppet, my codpiece, my shoe, my slipper, I shall never see you again! Ah, false death, how cruel and spiteful you are to me, robbing me of her who should have been immortal by right!

PLAY-LEADER: Saying this, he blubbered like a cow. But then, all of a sudden, he started laughing like a calf.

GARGANTUA: Ho, my little son, my little bollock, my little tootsie, how pretty you are! Ho, ho, ho, how happy I am! Let's drink, ho, and put away sadness. Bring some of my best wine, rinse the glasses, lay the cloth, light the candles, and make the soup.

(*The dirges for Badebec's funeral are heard.*)

Lord God, must I turn sad again? Weeping upsets me; I'm no longer young; I'm growing old; the times are dangerous.

Upon my word, it's better to weep less and drink more!

My wife is dead. She's well off; she's in paradise at least. She's praying to God for us; she's very happy; our troubles and calamities don't worry her any more. I must think about looking for another one.

(*The funeral procession approaches.*)

[(*Speaking to the others*): Go to her funeral, and in the meantime I'll stay here rocking my son. For I feel very poorly and might be in danger of falling ill. But have a good

drink beforehand. You'll feel all the better for it, believe me.]
(*While the funeral procession moves away he sings.*)

> Badebec is 'neath the earth
> Because she died while giving birth.
> Pray to God to take her in,
> And pardon her if she's in sin,
> She who drew her dying breath
> The year and day she suffered death.

SCENE TEN
Pantagruel's Childhood

FIRST ACTOR: It is hard to believe how quickly Pantagruel grew in body and strength. While still in his cradle he drank the milk of four thousand six hundred cows at every meal. [One day when they tried to get him to suck one of his cows, he broke free from one of the straps keeping him in the cradle, grasped the cow under the ham, and ate both her udders and half her belly, together with her liver and kidneys.]
(*Terrible bellows from the cow.*[1] *All gather around the animal, in the wings.*)

EXCLAMATIONS IN THE CROWD:

—— The poor cow! Listen to her bellowing!

(*From the wings, pieces of the cow are thrown on to the stage.*)

—— He's going to eat her up!

—— Get her away from him!

—— He's kept hold of the ham; he's eating it like a sausage!

—— Get the bone from him! Get the bone from him!

—— He's swallowing it like a cormorant swallowing a little fish!

[1] The rest of this scene was omitted from the Élysée-Montmartre production, which went on to Scene Twelve.

PANTAGRUEL'S VOICE (*recorded, echoing around the theatre*): Yum, yum!

PLAY-LEADER: Because he couldn't talk properly yet!

SCENE ELEVEN[1]

Concerning Rabelais and also Pantagruel's Education

The Orator is seated on a throne O.P. A hideous Jesuit is seated on a throne P.S. The rest of the company are centre-stage. The Play-Leader is walking up and down. The dialogue should be very brisk.

PLAY-LEADER: His father rejoiced to see him progressing visibly day by day. He sent him to Poitiers to study.

ORATOR: Then to the other universities of France: La Rochelle, Bordeaux, Toulouse.

A GIRL: Where he learned to dance very well.

PLAY-LEADER: But he didn't stay there for long when he saw that they burned heretics alive like red herrings.

(*Centre-stage, an actor is burnt at the stake in mime. Smoke.*)

THE DYING MAN: Good people, throw more wood on the fire! More wood!

A COMMENTATOR: The calves of his legs were roasting, his face was all black, and his tongue was swollen and protruding. His body was oozing fat and blood. The skin of his belly had burst and his bowels were escaping.

AN ACTOR: Yet he was still alive and beating his breast.

(*The dying man makes the sign of the Cross.*)

THE HIDEOUS JESUIT: Jesus! Jesus! Why do these young people insist on getting themselves burnt for nothing?

[1] This scene was omitted from the Élysée-Montmartre production.

MODERN ORATOR: Rabelais, for his part, was thirsty enough by nature without needing a fire to parch him.

PLAY-LEADER: He went to Montpellier and began studying medicine.

ORATOR: But after the confiscation of his Greek books he left the Franciscans. Thanks to the patronage of the humanists, he was taken in by the Benedictines.

PLAY-LEADER: He left Nîmes and travelled by way of the Pont du Gard to Avignon.

A GIRL: Where he fell in love before he had been there three days. For the women there love playing the two-backed beast, as Avignon is papal territory.

PLAY-LEADER: In view of this. . . .

ORATOR: He hastened to Lyons, an active centre thanks to its printing-houses. He divided his time between heretical publishers and the sick in the hospital.

A MAN: The greatest folly in the world is to think that there are stars for kings, popes, and great lords, but none for the poor and needy.

ORATOR: The "affair of the placards" burst upon France. Humanists and Protestants were persecuted. He took refuge in Dauphiné.

PLAY-LEADER: But the louts of the town used to beat up the students.

ORATOR: He disappeared. Left his order a second time. The Pope pardoned him.

PLAY-LEADER: With a hop, a skip and a jump, he arrived at Angers, but was driven away by the plague. So he went to Bourges, where he studied in the Faculty of Law.

ORATOR: Then to Orléans, where Calvin was studying.

PLAY-LEADER: And where he learnt to play tennis. But he was careful not to break his head with studying for fear that his sight might be affected.

A YOUNG MAN: For there is nothing so bad for the sight as weak eyes.

SCENE TWELVE
Paris

PLAY-LEADER: His father rejoiced to see him progressing visibly day by day. He decided to send him to the great university of Paris. (*A loud chord of music, and the rhythm changes. Solemn entry of Pantagruel and Epistemon. Pantagruel is François I as painted by Clouet, in a black and gold costume, and walking on lifts a foot high. While the actors go to meet him, staring at him in astonishment, the Play-Leader continues.*)

The people of Paris are so foolish, inquisitive and inept by nature, at every level of society, that a juggler, a carrier of relics, a mule with cymbals, or an organ-grinder in the middle of a crossroads, will bring together more people than a good gospel-preacher.

A GIRL: But isn't he a giant any more?

EPISTEMON: It all depends. He takes whatever form he likes.

PLAY-LEADER: Pantagruel studied very hard at the Library of Saint-Victor.

MEMBERS OF THE CHORUS (*brandishing books*):
—— Codpiece law,
—— the elephant's testicle,
—— flirtations among the Dominicans,
—— the art of farting decently in company,
—— the practice of flaying horses and mares.

PLAY-LEADER: His father wrote to him often.

GARGANTUA (*on a platform up-stage*):
My very dear son,
Neither in Plato's time, nor in Cicero's, were there such facilities for study as exist today. I find robbers, hangmen, freebooters and ostlers more learned nowadays than the doctors and preachers were in my time.

CHORUS (*continuing*):
—— the smelliness of Spaniards by Friar Inigo,
—— the worm-powders of the poor,
—— the history of hobgoblins,
—— the dishonesty of ecclesiastics.

GARGANTUA (*continuing*): But knowledge without conscience is but the ruin of the soul. It behoves you to serve, love and fear God; to put all your thoughts and hopes in Him; and to attach yourself to Him through faith and charity. Be suspicious of the evil practices of the world, and let no vanity enter your heart; for this life is transitory, but the word of God lasts for ever.

CHORUS (*continuing*):
—— the art of invoking male and female demons,
—— the donkey-pricks of priests,
—— the use of suppositories,
—— the pharmacopoeia of the soul.

GARGANTUA: Be helpful to all your neighbours and love them as yourself. Respect your tutors, shun the company of people you would not wish to resemble; and when you have acquired all the knowledge there is to be acquired, come home to me, so that I may see you and give you my blessing before I die.

My son, the peace and grace of Our Lord be with you.
Your father,
> Gargantua.

(*Gargantua fades into the darkness, for ever. Panurge has appeared centre-stage. Special lighting for him. Silence. Everyone turns to look at this strange individual.*)

PANTAGRUEL: Look at that man coming along the road from the Charenton bridge.

CHORUS (*each remark from a different person*):
—— Not too big, and not too small.
—— An aquiline nose, like the handle of a razor.
—— Sharp as a needle.
—— Quite handsome.
—— A bit of a lecher by the look of him, but otherwise the nicest fellow in the world.

EPISTEMON: But in such a sorry state that he looks as if he had been worried by a pack of hounds.

ANOTHER: He looks to me like an apple-picker from Perche.

PANTAGRUEL: By my faith, he is poor only in fortune, for I assure you that his face shows he comes of rich and noble stock.

Friend, be good enough to answer my questions: Who are you? Where do you come from? Where are you going? What are you looking for? And what is your name?

PANURGE (*in German*): Junker, Gott geb euch Glück und Hail. Die Gedechtnis des Klends und Armut vorlangst erlitten ist ein grosser Lust.

PANTAGRUEL: I don't understand that gibberish.

PANURGE (*in Arabic*): Al barildim gotfano dech min brin alabo dordin falbroth ringuam albaras.

PANTAGRUEL: Can you make anything of that?

EPISTEMON: It's the language of the Antipodes, and nobody can make head or tail of it.

PANURGE (*in Italian*): Signor mio, voi vedete per essempio che la cornamusa non suona mai s'ela non a il ventre pieno.

PANTAGRUEL: That's no better.

PANURGE (*in Scots*): Laird, if ye ken as much as ye look guid, you'll hae pity on me.

PANTAGRUEL: I understand that even less.

PANURGE (*in English, German and French, all mixed together*): Prug frest frinst sorgdmand strochdt drhds pag brlelang Gravot Chavigny Pomardière rustu pkakhdracg Devinière près Nays.

EPISTEMON: Once again, who are you? Where do you come from?

PANURGE: From the alme inclite Lemovic region.

EPISTEMON: I understood him that time! He's a Limousin!

PANURGE: As verisimulous amorabunds, we captate the benevolence of the omnijugal, omniform, omnigenous female sex.

PANTAGRUEL: Come now, friend, can't you speak honest-to-goodness French?

PANURGE: Why, yes, milord, very well. It's my native language and mother tongue, for I was born and bred as a boy in Touraine, the garden of France.

PANTAGRUEL: What is your name?

PANURGE: Milord, my true and proper Christian name is Panurge, and I have just come from Turkey, where I was taken prisoner. The Turks had put me on a spit, larded like a rabbit, and were beginning to roast me alive. . . .

I would be glad to tell you my story, for I've had adventures more amazing than those of Ulysses. But at the moment I feel an urgent need to eat. My teeth are sharp, my belly empty, my appetite enormous: for God's sake give me some food.

PANTAGRUEL: If you agree, I shall take you with me, and you shall never leave me.

EPISTEMON: Well said, and we'll leave this lousy university of Paris and its Saint Genevieve hill. The prisoners of the Moors and Tartars, the murderers in prison, even the dogs in your house are treated better than you are in these universities!

EUSTHENES: If I were King of Paris, I'd set fire to the university and burn both the Principal and the Regents who allow this inhumanity.

(*They start walking about. Change of lighting.*)

PANURGE: Just look at those fine walls!

EPISTEMON: They're very old: they go back to Philip Augustus.

PANURGE: By my beard, a cow could knock down more than forty feet of them with a single fart.

PANTAGRUEL: No town or city can have a stronger wall than the courage of its citizens. This city is so strong from the warlike host inside it that they don't need any other walls. Besides, if anyone wanted to wall Paris in, it wouldn't be possible, the cost would be so high.

PANURGE: All the same, it's good to have a stone wall around you when you're invaded by the enemy, if only to be able to ask: "Who is that, down there?" As for the enormous amount you say it would cost to wall in the city, if those gentlemen on the city council would grease my palm, I'd teach them a completely new method of building walls cheap.

PANTAGRUEL: What's that?

PANURGE: Don't breathe a word to a soul, and I'll tell you.

I've observed that the thingummies of the women of

Paris are cheaper than stones. They ought to be used to build the walls, arranged in good architectural symmetry, with the biggest in front and the rest sloping like a donkey's back, the middle-sized ones next and the little ones last. Then they ought to be joined together in a diamond pattern, as in the great tower at Bourges, by an equal number of stiff what's-their-names which inhabit monastic codpieces. What devil could possibly overthrow walls like that? There's no metal which could stand up to blows as well as they could. Besides, if any cannonballs came and rubbed against them, the juice of the great pox would spurt out straight away, like rain! I can see only one drawback to the idea.

PANTAGRUEL: And what's that?

PANURGE: There's nothing that flies like better.

PANTAGRUEL: Ho, ho, ha, ha, ha! But how do you know that women's private parts are so cheap in this city, where there are a great many chaste and modest women, and a great many virgins?

PANURGE: Why, because I've stuffed four hundred and seventeen of them since I arrived here, and I've only been here nine days.

SCENE THIRTEEN

Homeward Bound

Change of lighting. As they walk along they sing.

SONG: When Theo first slept with his bride
He laid a mallet by his side.
"What is this mallet, dear?" said she.
"To bash you with, my love," said he.
"Oh, come!" she said. "Don't be a fool,

68

Why do you need a wooden tool?
When Big John to my bed does come,
He bashes me with just his bum."
(*They are now in the open country.*)

PANTAGRUEL (*stopping suddenly to meditate*): Why are the leagues
in France so short compared with the leagues in other
countries? Do you know the reason, Panurge?

PANURGE: In ancient times, countries were not measured in
leagues, miles, stadia or parasangs until King Pharamond
divided them up in the following way. (*Panurge's explana-
tion is illustrated by a graceful "pas de deux".*)

He picked a hundred handsome, gallant young men in
Paris and a hundred pretty Picardy girls, and had them well
fed for a week. Then he called them before him, gave each
young man his girl with plenty of money for expenses, and
ordered them to go off in different directions. At every spot
where they played the two-backed beast with their girls, they
were to set up a stone—and that should be a league.

So the young fellows set off in high spirits, and because
they were fresh and rested, they took their pleasure at the
end of every field, which is why the leagues in France are so
short.

But when they had gone a long way and were devilish
tired, they didn't play the ram so often, and contented
themselves—I'm talking of the men—with one wretched
bout a day.

And that's why the leagues in Brittany, Germany and
other countries even farther away are so long. (*End of
dance.*)

PANURGE (*to the audience*): Other people give other reasons, but
I think that one's best.

(*The stage grows darker. Thunder in the distance.*)

EPISTEMON: Do you see that big raincloud in the sky?

PANURGE: Let's all huddle together.

MODERN ORATOR: Charles V and François I have patched up their
differences at Aigues-Mortes. And that means more
repression and persecution!

PANTAGRUEL: It's nothing. It won't be anything more than a

shower. But just in case, huddle up close and I'll cover you with my tongue, like a hen covering her chickens.[1]

SCENE FOURTEEN[2]
Pantagruel's Throat[3]

Thunder. Lightning. Pantagruel's tongue unfolds on to the stage, which by means of projectors and machinery is transformed into his throat. All except Panurge take refuge under the tongue, almost disappearing underneath. Panurge is inquisitive and explores the throat. Rumblings in the background (musique concrète).

PANURGE: O gods and goddesses, what do I see here? Huge rocks —those must be his teeth—vast meadows, great forests, and fortified towns like Lyons or Poitiers. (*He takes a drink from his flagon, to raise his spirits. He notices a man gardening.*) Friend, what are you doing here?

THE MAN: I'm planting cabbages.

PANURGE: But what for?

THE MAN: Why, sir, we can't all sit around with heavy balls like lazy folk. I earn my living like this, and take my cabbages to sell in the market in the town back there.

PANURGE: Jesus, is there a *new world* here?

THE MAN: Oh, it isn't new at all. Outside they say there's a *new found land*, with a sun and a moon, but this one is older.

PANURGE: What's the name of this town of yours?

THE MAN: It's called Gullet Town, and they're all Christians there, and decent folk, who'll give you a warm welcome.

[1] For a stage performance, continue with Panurge's final speech in Scene Fourteen.
[2] This scene was omitted from the Élysée-Montmartre production.
[3] The first appearance of the fantastic, and the only time projectors are used in Part One.

(*Panurge has another drink. A second man appears with some pigeons.*)

PANURGE: Friend, where do these pigeons come from?

SECOND MAN: Sir, they come from *the other world*. When the gate here yawns open, they fly inside in great flocks.

(*He disappears, and his pigeons fly away. Panurge has another drink and paces up and down uneasily.*)

A GATEKEEPER: Can I see your bill of health?

PANURGE: Why, is there a risk of the plague here?

GATEKEEPER: O, milord, they are dying so fast in here that the corpse cart is never off the streets.

PANURGE: Good God! And where's this?

GATEKEEPER: In the towns of Larynx and Pharynx. A foul, stinking exhalation keeps coming up from the abyss, and in the last week it has killed twenty-two hundred and sixty thousand and sixteen people (not counting the women and children).

They call it the garlic plague, or garlicitis, and I don't advise you to go there. But if you climb those rocks over there, you'll find the finest scenery in all the world—beautiful meadows, plenty of vines, and fields full of flowers.

PANURGE (*taking another drink*): And farther down, by the back teeth?

GATEKEEPER: In the underlips? Watch out for the brigands who come down from the ears.

PANURGE (*taking another drink*): And how do people earn their living here?

GATEKEEPER: By sleeping. People are hired by the day just to sleep, and paid five or six sous a day. Those who can snore very loud are paid a good seven and a half.

PANURGE: And I suppose that, just as we have hilldwellers and plaindwellers, you have toothdwellers and gumdwellers.

They're certainly right when they say that one half of the world doesn't know how the other half lives. . . . But I must go back now. (*He drains his flagon, and walks down-stage while the lighting changes.*)

PANTAGRUEL'S VOICE (*recorded*): Where have you been, Panurge?

PANURGE (*looking up in the air*): Down your throat, milord.

PANTAGRUEL'S VOICE (*recorded*): And what did you live on down there?

PANURGE: On the same food as you, milord. I charged a toll on the tastiest morsels that came my way.

PANTAGRUEL'S VOICE (*recorded*): Ha, ha, you're a good fellow, and no mistake. I'm going to give you the Wardenship of Salmagundy.

PANURGE: Many thanks, milord. You're giving me more than my deserts.

PANTAGRUEL'S VOICE (*recorded*): Your dessert, Panurge, your dessert! Ha, ha, ha!

(*Enormous rumblings. The recorded voice fades away. The throat décor recedes to the sound of music and a few last rumbles. Panurge remains alone.*)

PANURGE (*to the audience, holding the empty flagon in his hand*): My head's aching and I can feel that the registers of my brain have been a little confused by this Septembral juice.

PANURGE:[1] What a good idea! Let's disappear for a while. (*To the audience.*) You'll have the rest of the story in a few minutes.

So good-bye for the moment, ladies and gentlemen. *Perdonate mi.* And don't worry about my faults any more than you do about your own. If you say to me: "It isn't very wise of you to show us all this idle nonsense," I'll reply that you're no wiser listening to it.

But if you came here for amusement, then you and I both deserve forgiveness more than a lot of bigots, prudes, hypocrites, cheats and creeps, grumps and grousers, who put on disguises like mummers to deceive the world. (*All the house lights come on suddenly, and the sound of bottles and glasses comes from the bar....*)

INTERVAL

[1] For the stage production: continued from Scene Thirteen.

PART TWO

Panurge
and the Voyage

THE ABBEY OF THELEMA[1]

SCENE ONE

"Under the Laurels"

Friar John of the Funnels is bustling about, very much the master of the house. The atmosphere is relaxed, with the women wearing very low-cut dresses, "some open lower than the bosom" (Éloy d'Amerval). Youths with provocative codpieces are improvising dances with their girls. "Hippy" couples are lying here and there, making "love not war". Musicians are playing.

On a throne on the left sits the Play-Leader.

On a throne on the right a theologian (Putherbeus) sits dozing, with the jester Triboulet at his feet.

In the centre are Pantagruel, Epistemon, Gymnast, Eusthenes, Carpalim and Xenomanes.

BOYS AND GIRLS (*singing and dancing*):
Let's dance and frolic, love and play,
Let's drink wine flowing from the tun,
We do nothing every day
But gambol gaily in the sun.
(*Panurge, very excited in this sequence, pursues an attractive young lady.*)

PANURGE: Madam, this journey has warmed the cockles of my
. . . heart. It would be most beneficial to the State, delightful to you, an honour for your progeny, and necessary for
me, that I should cover you and propagate my line.

[1] The Abbey of Thelema should reveal complete freedom of expression, with each person improvising in harmony with the ideas of the others. Pantagruel's group is relaxed, enjoying the harmony of humanist pleasure. Only Panurge is excited, as neophytes tend to be. The girls should be very sexy, and the boys should look rather like beatniks.

75

Look, here's Master John Thomas asking for lodging.
He's a frisky fellow, who can find his way into every nook
and cranny in your rat-trap. So to save time let's open up
and heave-ho!
(*The lady runs away.*)

PANTAGRUEL: Panurge, Panurge, come here! Dress him in my livery.
(*While Panurge's costume is being changed, the music and
dancing continue.*)

PANURGE: A coat of arms for me!
They asked: What shall it be?
I said: Really, what'll
It be but a bottle?
That's just the thing for me!

Now be careful about the codpiece. I want a codpiece
three foot long, and square at the end, not round. If there's
one thing I hate it's a round codpiece. So barbaric! So
gothic!

When I have a little time to myself, I'm going to write a
book about codpieces: a book with a long tailpiece. . . .
(*While he is being dressed in his new livery, the pockets of his
old costume are emptied.*)

PANTAGRUEL: What's this whip?

PANURGE: That's for warming the legs of any page I find carrying
wine to his master—to speed him on his way.

PANTAGRUEL: And this little pointed knife?

PANURGE: That's for cutting purses open.

PANTAGRUEL: And this flask of vinegar?

PANURGE: That's for the soldiers of the watch, to throw in their
eyes.

PANTAGRUEL: You're a real rapscallion, aren't you? And what are
these burning-mirrors for?

PANURGE: Those are for shining on any woman in church who's
looking a bit down-in-the-mouth. You know the saying: If
she's sad at the Mass, she's mad in the ass.

PANTAGRUEL: And these boxes of fleas and lice?

PANURGE: Those are to put down the backs of shrews and bigots
to make them scratch themselves in public or run through
the streets. (*He starts running after the pretty lady again.*)

Madam, I'm so enamoured of you that I can neither piss
nor shit for love of you.

THE LADY: I want nothing to do with you, sir.

PANURGE: I want something to do with you though. Pray God,
Madam, that He grant me what your noble heart desires.

THE LADY: Really, sir! (*She runs away.*)

THE OTHERS: Panurge! Panurge! Panurge!
(*Panurge's pockets have now been completely emptied.*)

PANTAGRUEL: Panurge, you look to me like a sick man, and I
know the name of your sickness: diarrhoea of the purse.

FRIAR JOHN (*humming*): "Of all ailments there's none worse
Than a loosening of the purse."

PANURGE (*turning out his pockets*): That's my sickness, all right.
Mind you, I've often had a few crowns to my name, but
they've always gone to somebody else's.

"Oh, where are the snows of yesteryear?" That's what
worried François Villon, the poet.

PANTAGRUEL: I have appointed you Warden of Salmagundy,
Panurge, and that should give you a regular income.

PANURGE: Not to mention an irregular income from snails and
maybugs. . . .

PANTAGRUEL: What worries me is the fear that you'll spend all
your money and eat your wheat in the blade.

PANURGE: Eat my wheat in the blade? Why, that's like the
hermit who lives on salads and roots.

After all, who can tell whether the world will last another
three years? And even if it lasted longer than that, is there
any man fool enough to count on three years of life?
(*He declaims*): [No one but a god can say
Whether he'll live another day.

As for wheat in the blade, you can make a fine green
sauce from it, simple to mix and easy to digest, which
stimulates the brain, exhilarates the animal spirits, rejoices
the sight, rouses the appetite, delights the taste, fortifies the
heart, tickles the tongue, clears the complexion, strengthens
the muscles, tempers the blood, eases the diaphragm,
refreshes the liver, unblocks the spleen, relieves the kidneys,
relaxes the loins, tones up the vertebrae, empties the ureters,

dilates the spermatic vessels, tightens the testicle strings, purges the bladder, swells the genitals, adjusts the foreskin, hardens the glands, rectifies the member, sets your tool upright, and lots of other rare advantages.] (*Panurge circles around the lady again.*)

PANTAGRUEL: But when will you be out of debt?

PANURGE: When all the world is happy.

A world without debts? Why, if that ever comes about, there'll be chaos in the heavens. [Jupiter will forget his debt to Saturn and rob him of his sphere. Then Saturn will join with Mars and together they'll turn our world upside down.]

The moon will remain in darkness, and the Sun will shed no more light on earth. Earth will not turn into water, water will not be transmuted into air, air will not make fire, and fire will not warm earth. In man too, the head will refuse to lend the sight of its eyes to guide the hands and feet. The feet will not deign to carry it, the hands will cease to work for it, and the heart will throw up its job. And in that disorderly world where nothing will be owed, nothing lent, nothing borrowed, the body will suddenly rot, and the soul will go to the devil.

[Among men, nobody will save his neighbour. Nobody will go to another's help. Why? Because he has nothing to lend, and nobody owes him anything. Faith, Hope and Charity will be banished from that world, for men are born to help and succour one another.]

PANTAGRUEL: What a preacher! What a sermonizer! Go on.

PANURGE: If you insist. Now imagine, on the contrary, another world in which everybody lends and everybody owes, where all are debtors and all are lenders. Oh, what harmony there will be, what sympathy between the elements! I can already imagine myself living there! And consider our microcosm, I mean that little world which is man. It was our creator's intention to house the soul and maintain life in it. Now life consists of blood, and blood is the seat of the soul. Nature provides the material best suited to be turned into blood: bread and wine.

78

To find this food, prepare it and cook it, the hands work, the feet move, the eyes guide. When it is ready, the tongue tries it, the teeth chew it, the stomach receives it and digests it and chylifies it. The veins suck out of it what is good, leaving the excrements to be expelled, and carries it to the liver, which promptly turns it into blood.

The heart, by its diastolic and systolic movements, refines and heats it to such a degree that it sends it to all the members. Each member absorbs it and feeds on it after its own fashion. And thus feet, hands, eyes, and all the rest become debtors who were previously lenders.

PANTAGRUEL (*laughing*): No man is so rich that he doesn't sometimes owe money. And no man is so poor that you can't borrow from him at times.

PANURGE (*exultantly*): And that isn't all. This lending, owing, borrowing world is so good that when all this feeding is over, it starts thinking of lending to those who are not yet born: the children of the future.

For that purpose every member selects and puts aside part of the best of its nourishment, and sends it below. There Nature has prepared suitable vessels and receptacles for it, through which it descends to the genitals by long circuitous routes, to find fitting form and suitable places, in both man and woman, for the conservation and perpetuation of the human race. All this is done by loans and debts from one to the other.

God's faith, I drown, I perish, I lose my way when I enter the depths of that world of lenders and owers. It is a divine thing, not to take and receive, but to extend and give. (*He almost swoons in the lady's arms. There is a silence, then desire takes hold of Panurge again.*)

[CARPALIM: What's that ring you are wearing, Panurge?

EPISTEMON: In the right ear, Jewish fashion?

EUSTHENES: With a flea set in the bezel?]

PANURGE: I've got a flea in my ear! I want to get married! What do you think of the idea, milord?

PANTAGRUEL: If the die is cast and your mind made up, then all that remains is to carry out your decision.

PANURGE: But I wouldn't like to carry it out without your advice.

PANTAGRUEL: Then I advise you to get married.

PANURGE: You know the saying: *Vae soli!* Woe to him who is alone. A man on his own never has as much pleasure as you see married people having.

PANTAGRUEL: Then get married.

PANURGE: But if my wife made me a cuckold that would make me fly off my hinges.

PANTAGRUEL: Then don't get married.

PANURGE: But since I can't do without a woman, any more than a blind man can do without a stick—for the old cock has to be kept busy, otherwise I couldn't live—wouldn't it be better for me to set up house with some decent, virtuous woman?

PANTAGRUEL: Then get married.

PANURGE: But if I married a worthy woman and she beat me—and I've heard tell that those women of the world usually have very bad tempers—I'd give her such a thrashing that the great Devil himself would come to the door of Hell to wait for her damned soul.

PANTAGRUEL: Then don't get married. . . .

PANURGE: But without getting married I could never have any legitimate sons and daughters that I can have fun with as good folk do in the privacy of their homes.

PANTAGRUEL: Then for God's sake get married!

PANURGE: Your advice, if I may say so, changes from one minute to the next.

PANTAGRUEL: But there are so many ifs and buts in your arguments. Aren't you sure of what you *will*? That's the main thing: all the rest is by the way and depends on the inexorable dispositions of heaven.

FRIAR JOHN (*who has been consulting a copy of Virgil in accordance with the practice of the times*): I've just consulted this copy of Virgil by putting my finger in three times, and I find that you'll be cuckolded, beaten and robbed.

PANURGE: Should I get married, then, Friar John?

FRIAR JOHN (*losing patience with him*): Yes, damn you, get married, and ring out a double peal on your balls! And the

quicker the better! Get the banns called and the bed
creaking this very night. In God's name what are you
waiting for? Didn't you say that the end of the world was
drawing near? Do you want to be found with your balls full
on Judgement Day?

PANURGE: You have a clear, serene mind, Friar John, you
metropolitan ball-bag, and you speak to the point. Such a
precious substance shouldn't be wasted.

FRIAR JOHN: But time undermines everything. There's no bronze
or marble that isn't subject to old age and decay. I can see
the hair on your head turning grey already. By my thirst,
my old friend, when there's snow on the mountain—I mean
the head and chin—there's not much heat in the valleys of
the codpiece.

PANURGE: When there's snow on the mountain, there's thunder
and lightning and all the devils of hell in the valleys. You
poke fun at my greying hair, but you forget it's like a leek.
You see, a leek's got a white head, but its tail is green and
strong and straight.

FRIAR JOHN: My old friend, it's not everybody who can be a
cuckold. And if you're a cuckold, *ergo* your wife will be
beautiful, *ergo* she'll treat you well, *ergo* you'll have plenty
of friends, *ergo* you'll be saved. So there, you mouldy old
ball-bag.

But if you like, I'll tell you a way of preventing your wife
from ever making you a cuckold without your consent.

PANURGE: By the soul of my red-hot codpiece, I'm listening to
you, you velvety ball-bag.

FRIAR JOHN (*going into the auditorium*): Hans Carvel was a learned,
skilful, studious, worthy man, a man of good sense and
sound judgement, good-humoured, charitable, generous and
philosophical. He was a merry fellow too, a good companion and a great joker. In his old age he married the
bailiff's daughter, who was young and beautiful, dainty and
flirtatious, and a little too charming to his neighbours and
his servants, so that he became as jealous as a tiger, and
began to suspect her of getting her buttocks slapped somewhere else. To prevent this from happening, he told her

dozens of fine stories about the misfortunes caused by adultery, read her the legend of the chaste women, and preached the virtues of modesty to her.

In spite of all this, he found her so wilful and merry with his neighbours that he grew more and more jealous. Then, one night, when he was lying in bed with her, he dreamt that he was talking to the devil and telling him his grievances. The devil comforted him and put a ring on his middle finger, saying: "I will give you this ring. As long as you wear it on your finger, no man will have carnal relations with your wife without your knowledge and consent." "Many thanks, Master Devil," said Hans Carvel. "I'll renounce Mahomet if anybody ever takes it off my finger."

The devil disappeared, and Hans Carvel woke up thoroughly delighted, to find that he had his finger in his wife's thingummyjig. When his wife felt it, she pulled her bottom away, saying: "Oh, no, that's not what you should put in there."

Believe me, always do like Hans Carvel and keep your wife's ring on your finger! (*While Friar John is returning towards Panurge, his recorded voice is heard.*)

> He wakes with the first morning breeze
> And is horrified by what he sees,
> For his finger all night
> Has been stuck really tight
> In his wife's you-know-what, if you please.[1]

(*Triboulet, who all this time has been wandering around, eating an apple or playing with a pig's bladder, rushes up to Panurge. He takes a swig of wine, thumps Panurge on the back, hands him the bottle, slaps his face with the pig's bladder, and wags his head violently.*)

CARPALIM: Watch out! Our fool is going into an ecstasy.

PANTAGRUEL (*while Triboulet is waving his hands about*): Gestures are the language of the fingers. Nothing could be truer than that.

EPISTEMON: The spirit of prophecy has taken hold of him.

EUSTHENES: See how he's wagging his head! Let's listen to his prophecy!

[1] From the *conte* by La Fontaine 'taken from Rabelais'.

(Triboulet goes into a positive ecstasy.)

TRIBOULET: By God—God—crazy fool—beware of the monk! The bagpipe of Buzançay! *(He waves the pig's bladder, draws his sword, and tries to strike Panurge with it. He is pulled away.)*

FRIAR JOHN: "Beware of the monk!" he said. That means you'll be cuckolded by some monk. And that's the most infamous sort of cuckoldry.

PANURGE: That isn't the crux of the matter. He handed me the bottle, and I swear by the Styx and Acheron in your presence that I won't wear a codpiece on my breeches until I've consulted the Oracle of the Holy Bottle. Let's go there together! I beg you to take me there!

PANTAGRUEL: It's a long journey, full of risks and dangers.

PANURGE: What dangers? Dangers fly from me for twenty miles around. Xenomanes, my friend, you who love travelling in foreign parts, give us your advice.

XENOMANES: We should have to pass through Lanternland.

PANTAGRUEL: So be it. Let us fit out a ship in our port of Thalassa, near Saint-Malo. Xenomanes, great traveller that you are, and navigator of perilous seas, be our guide! *(Music.)*

FRIAR JOHN *(consulting his copy of Virgil)*: My Virgil says: "Flee these cruel lands, flee these arid shores!"

THE VOYAGE

Fitting Out

While Pantagruel's ship is being fitted out, and the Abbey of Thelema is disappearing, there is music and a sound of hammering. The words form part of the music.

CHORUS: Mariners. Pilots. Boatswains. Interpreters. Craftsmen. Soldiers. Provisions. Artillery. Munitions. Clothing. Money.

And we are all taking on board a great quantity of Pantagruelion.

The herb Pantagruelion has a small, hard, round, blunt white root.

Long live hemp!

Hard, rough, green leaves, with sickle-shaped edges.

Long live hemp!

(*In various parts of the stage, actors appear to be suffering from the effects of hashish. The word "hashish" can be heard.*)

Too much of it makes bad blood, harms the brain with excessive heat, fills the head with noxious vapours.

Long live hemp!

It is sown at the coming of the swallows and pulled out of the ground when the cicadas grow hoarse.

ALL: Long live hemp!

Indians, Arabs and Sabaeans,
Sing no longer hymns and paeans
To incense, myrrh or ebony.
Come here our nobler plant to see.
Take home its seed at any rate

And see if it will propagate,
And if it takes, give thanks a million
To the land of Pantagruelion.
Long live hemp!
(*Religious music as the voyage begins.*
Xenomanes, who looks like Jacques Cartier, traces the route
they are going to follow with a long pointer on a transparent
map. A drawing of China, bearing the names of Magellan and
Jacques Cartier.)

XENOMANES: The Oracle of the Holy Bottle lies near Cathay, in
Upper India. Now I don't intend to take the route usually
taken by the Portuguese, who sail through the torrid zone
and round the Cape of Good Hope at the southern tip of
Africa. We shall sail round the Pole in a westerly direction.

The time is right. Let us set sail with a south-easterly
wind behind us.

ALL ON BOARD: Here's a health to you all!
(*Actors and attendants distribute glasses of white wine among*
the audience.)

ALL ON SHORE: Good health! Godspeed!
(*Music. Pantagruel's ship, the* Thalamege, *emerges down-*
stage, P.S. The music becomes quieter, then stops.)

SCENE THREE

Calumny

MODERN ORATOR: The time is far from right, and the wind is
blowing towards exile. Rabelais has to flee to Metz, an
imperial city but one where French is spoken. Charles V has
won over the Pope.

François I disappears. The Papists and Sorbonicoles, the
lawyers and judges, the Inquisition and the Jesuits are
victorious.

His books are condemned, in spite of all the joy, comfort and consolation they afford.

(*Calvin has taken his place on the left-hand throne, Putherbeus[1] on the right-hand throne.*)

PUTHERBEUS: Drive that buffoon out of France! To Geneva with him!

ORATOR: But Calvin rails against him too.

CALVIN: His soul is no different from a dog or a pig.

ORATOR: Henceforth his life will be nothing but a long voyage through criticisms, condemnations, ambushes and hypocrisy, from which he will escape by means of trickery, flight or exile, to remain faithful to himself.

SCENE FOUR

The Sheep

Pantagruel's ship reappears. Music. Another ship comes towards it.[2]

XENOMANES: Look what's coming towards us.

SAILORS (*on both ships*):

—— Hard a-port! Hard a-port!

—— Ahoy there! Ahoy!

—— What news of the sea?

—— What news of *terra firma*?

—— What's happening in the world?

—— Where do you come from?

—— Lanternland!

—— Let's get together!

---

[1] This is Gabriel de Puits-Herbault, one of Rabelais's fiercest critics.

[2] Dingdong's boat, which is covered with sheepskins. Dingdong is dressed in a sheepskin and a little pointed hat, so that he looks like a white clown. This scene is a circus turn which has a cruel side to it. When the skins are all thrown overboard and everybody follows them the ship disappears too.

(The two ships tie up together. While the two companies are moving from one ship to the other, they continue.)

———— We are Frenchmen from Saintonge.

———— We are simple, stupid folk, but goodhearted for all that.

———— The Lanterns are a handsome, decent, jolly people.

———— They'll treat you very well.

———— They speak the French of Touraine.

———— What's happening over there?

(For Dingdong and Panurge are beginning to quarrel, because Dingdong has been making fun of Panurge's spectacles.)

PANURGE: You watch out, because my glasses help me to hear better than you think.

DINGDONG: You look a real cuckold, with no codpiece to your breeches!

PANURGE: Now how the devil could I be a cuckold, seeing that I'm not married yet, as you are, judging by your ugly mug?

DINGDONG: I've got one of the most beautiful, charming, virtuous and respectable wives in the whole of Saintonge. And I'm taking her a lovely eleven-inch branch of red coral as a present. But what's that got to do with you? What are you interfering for? You four-eyed son of Antichrist!

PANURGE: Tell me now: if, with the consent and connivance of the elements, I happened to have thingummyjiggered your beautiful, charming, virtuous and respectable wife, what would you do about it? Answer me, you pimping son of Mahomet!

DINGDONG: I'd slit you open with this sword and kill you like a ram. *(He tries to draw his sword, but without success.)*

PANURGE: Help! Help!

EPISTEMON: It's stuck in the scabbard with rust. Everything goes rusty at sea.

FRIAR JOHN: By my cutlass, he'd better not harm Panurge!

THE CAPTAIN OF DINGDONG'S SHIP: I want no trouble in my ship.

PANTAGRUEL: Shake hands and patch up your quarrel.

PANURGE *(to Epistemon and Friar John)*: Stand a little way off and you'll enjoy what you're going to see. This is going to be great fun, if nothing goes wrong. *(To Dingdong.)* Friend, you've got some fine sheep there! Will you sell me one?

DINGDONG: You're a crafty one, friend, tricking poor folk like
that. You look more like a cutter of purses than a dealer in
sheep.

PANURGE: Patience! Sell me one of your sheep. How much do you
want?

DINGDONG: What are you talking about, neighbour? These are
long-haired Levantine sheep, pedigree sheep, fatted sheep!

PANURGE: All right—I believe you. But for heaven's sake sell me
one.

DINGDONG: Friend, the fleeces of these sheep will be made into
fine Rouen cloth. The skins will be made into beautiful
moroccos. The guts will be made into violin and harp
strings. Now what do you think of that?

PANURGE: Please sell me one. Look: I'll pay cash.

DINGDONG: Friend, they are meat for none but kings and princes.
Their flesh is so tender, so savoury and so tasty that it's
like balm. I'm bringing them from a country where the very
pigs, God help us, eat nothing but myrobalan plums. When
the sows are in litter, they are fed on nothing but orange
blossom.

PANURGE: For God's sake, how much?

DINGDONG: In all the fields they piss in, the corn springs up as
if God Himself had pissed there. There's no need for marl
or manure.

    With their turds—pardon my language—the doctors in
our part of the world cure seventy-eight kinds of illness. So
they cost me a pretty penny.

PANURGE: Never mind how much they cost you. Just sell me one
and I'll pay you a good price for it.

DINGDONG: Now take those horns there and pound them with an
iron pestle. Then bury them in a sunny spot and water
them often. In a few months you'll see the best asparagus
in the world spring up.

PANURGE: Patience! But let's hurry up!

DINGDONG: And when I've paid proper tribute, friend and
neighbour, to the innards: the shoulders, the legs, the neck,
the breast, the liver, the spleen, the tripes, the bowels, the
bladder, the ribs. . . .

THE SHIP'S CAPTAIN: A turd on it! This haggling's gone on long enough. Sell it to him if you want to; but if you don't want to, stop fooling about with him.

DINGDONG: I will then, just to please you. But he'll pay me three pounds for it, and he can take his pick.

PANURGE: That's a lot of money. Still, here you are. (*Panurge then chooses a fine sheep. Its bleating is echoed by all the other sheep, making a tremendous din.*)

DINGDONG: Oh, he's made a good choice! He knows what he's doing, the rascal! Let's have a drink!

FRIAR JOHN: That's right! Let's have a drink!

(*Panurge, without saying a word, throws his crying, bleating sheep overboard. All the other sheep, crying and bleating on the same note, jump after it one after another. The din becomes infernal, with the bleating of sheep and the shouting of men.*) (*Description of the mime.*) The sheep were jostling with one another to be the first to jump overboard after their companion. It was impossible to hold them back, for as you know, it is the nature of sheep to follow their leader, wherever he may go.

The dealer, appalled by what was happening, tried to stop them and hold them back with all his might, but in vain. They all jumped into the sea and perished. Finally he grabbed a big strong one by the fleece on the forward deck, but the sheep was so strong that it pulled the dealer overboard with it, and he was drowned. The other shepherds and drovers did likewise, grabbing the sheep, some by the horns, others by the legs, and yet others by the fleece; and they were all likewise dragged into the sea and drowned miserably.

Panurge, holding an oar in one hand, not to help the drovers, but to prevent them from clambering aboard and escaping death, preached to them eloquently, pointing out to them in rhetorical language the miseries of this world and the felicities of the next.

PANURGE (*killing off those who are trying to clamber aboard*): The dead are happier than those who live in this vale of misery! (*The ships draw apart and Dingdong's ship disappears.*)

I do believe there isn't a sheepish soul left on board. What do you think of that, Friar John?

FRIAR JOHN: You did well. But you should have deferred payment, and the money would have stayed in your purse.

PANURGE: Oh, shit the money. I've had enough fun for fifty thousand pounds. Listen to me, Friar John. Nobody ever did me a good turn without getting a reward. I'm not an ungrateful man. But nobody ever did me a bad turn without regretting it. I'm not a fool either.

FRIAR JOHN: "*Mihi vindictam.*" Vengeance is mine, saith the Lord. That's Holy Writ, that is.

SCENE FIVE

The Storm[1]

Music heralding a storm. Wind effects.

EPISTEMON (*to Pantagruel*): Milord, you seem pensive and melancholy. Why this sadness, which is not like you?

XENOMANES: See how the weather-pennant's fluttering. That's a bad sign, and I can see a terrible squall coming.
(*The sea swells, the wind rises. From now on, words are used musically.*)
All hands on deck!
Haul down the sails!
Strike the bowlines!
Lower the mizzen-mast!
Bring down the yards!

---

[1] For the storm the whole theatre becomes the ship. The actors go out into the auditorium. Rigging falls from the ceiling, and projectors are used to give the audience the impression that they are on board the ship. Throughout this scene recorded storm sounds are used, with suitable lighting effects.

(The wind rises. Rain, squalls, thunder, lightning. In the following text the words on the left are chiefly for musical effect. Only those on the right should be clearly intelligible.)

XENOMANES AND OTHERS *(intermittently, above the din)*: It's a
   nor'wester. Here comes the hurricane.

Black squalls
Terrible gusts
Deadly scuds
Lightning
Rain
Hail

   The sky has lost its brightness. No light except from the
   lightning.

Flashes ripping the fiery clouds.
Blasts, flurries, simoons,
aerial ejaculations.

   The Chaos of old has returned, with air, sea and earth
   warring together!

PANTAGRUEL *(to whom Xenomanes has entrusted the helm)*: Let us
   implore the aid of the great God our Protector.
   *(Friar John, Epistemon and Ponocrates help the sailors, but
   Panurge squats on the deck, vomiting.)*

PANURGE: The saints protect us! Would to God and the blessed,
   worthy, holy Virgin that I were on dry land just now! O
   thrice blessed and four times blessed are those who plant
   cabbages! They've always got one foot on the ground and
   the other not far from it. O cruel Fates, why didn't you
   spin me a cabbage-planter's life? Believe me, there's nothing
   better to walk on than good honest cow-dung.

THE OTHERS: Halyards broken, cable in pieces, thimbles splitting,
manger falling in the sea, keel in the air. *Alles verloren!*
Done for! Our foremast! Adrift!

PANURGE: It's all up with me. I'm shitting myself with fear.
Boo, boo, boo, boo, boo, boo!
Otto, to, to, to, to, to, to, ti!
Boo, boo, boo, boo, boo, boo,
oo, oo, boo, boo, boo, boo!
   I'm drowning, I'm drowning, I'm drowned!

FRIAR JOHN: Panurge the calf, Panurge the blubberer, Panurge the whimperer.

PANURGE: Friar John, my dear friend, my dear father.

Be, be, be, boo, boo, boo.

I'm drowning, I'm drowning.

My friend, I'm drowning. It's all up with me, my father in God. Alas, alack! The water's got into my shoes through my collar.

Boo, boo, boo, pish,

hoo, hoo, hoo, ha, ha, ha,

ha, ha, I'm drowning. Alas,

alack, hoo, hoo, hoo, hoo, hoo,

hoo! Bebe, boo, boo, boboo,

boboo, ho, ho, ho, ho, ho, ho.

Alas, alack!

Friar John, my father and friend, hear my confession! Confiteor. . . .

FRIAR JOHN: In the name of thirty legions of devils, come here and help us.

PANURGE: Let's not swear, my father and friend, not now at any rate. Tomorrow we'll swear as much as you like.

Be, be, be, be, be,

boo, boo, boo, boo.

FRIAR JOHN: Magna, magna, magna! Isn't he a sight, the shitten blubberer? (*To a cabin-boy.*) Hey, there, boy! Lend us a hand!

PANURGE: I've swallowed over eighteen bucketfuls of water.

Boo, boo, boo, boo.

It's all salty and bitter.

XENOMANES:

Helm a-lee, ho! Helm a-lee!

Hands to the halyards!

Halyards! About ships with

her! Helm a-lee! Stand off

from the boom! Belay there!

Make fast below! Helm a-lee!

Head on to the sea!

Unhelm the tiller! Let her ride!

Let her ride!

(A great roll which almost capsizes the ship.)

PANTAGRUEL: Have we come to that? May Our Lord and Saviour protect us!

XENOMANES:

Let her ride!

Let every man think of his soul and start praying! Only a miracle can save us now!

FRIAR JOHN: Over here, by all the devils! To starboard! Let her ride, for God's sake!

Let her ride! Let her ride!

(A great clap of thunder.)

God Almighty, what thunder and hail! Hold fast there! Today's the feast of all the devils.

PANURGE: Friar John's damning himself in advance! Oh, what a good friend I'm losing in him!

Alas, alack!

PANTAGRUEL: Lord God, save us. But if we perish, thy will be done.

(Enormous clap of thunder. Everyone falls on the deck.)

PANURGE:

Bebe, boo, bebe, boo, boo.

Consummatum est. I forgive everyone.

FRIAR JOHN:

Magna, magna, magna!

(Rays of eerie light.)

PANTAGRUEL: Look, my lads! The sky's beginning to clear to the north. Pluck up your courage.

XENOMANES: Courage, my lads! The swell's dying down.

Hands to the maintop!

Man the capstan!

Clear the bowlines!

Tack to port!

Helm a-lee!

Hoist!

Hoist!

Heave!

Heave!

Right the helm!

A SAILOR: Right it is!

XENOMANES: Heave-ho, my lads! We've got our devils on the run. Gently does it.

Here, Gymnast, you lucky fornicator! All his brats will be boys, the lecher! Eusthenes, up to the foretop with you!

Hey, hey, it's a holiday! Noel, Noel!

EPISTEMON: I like that song. And today *is* a holiday.

XENOMANES: Let's drink to the fair weather!

PANURGE: By Saint John, that was well said! Oh, very well said!

FRIAR JOHN: If you taste a drop of wine after this, may the devil taste my blood. Do you hear that, you devil's ball-bag?

(*The storm is over. Food and drink are brought on deck.*)

PANTAGRUEL: Now, my lads, let's not fall out!

FRIAR JOHN: It's this poor devil Panurge who's got the shivers. He always shakes with fear when he's pissed.

PANTAGRUEL: If he was afraid during that storm, so long as he did his best to help, I don't think any the less of him. To be afraid all the time is a sign of a cowardly heart, but not to be afraid when there's every reason for fear is a sign of stupidity.

God be praised, nobody has died. And now we must repair this damage.

PANURGE: All's well. The storm's over. Can I help you over there? Let me coil that rope. What, aren't you doing anything, Friar John? Is this a time to sit around drinking? Hey there, sailor, let's have a word with you! How thick are the planks of this ship?

THE SAILOR: They're a good two inches thick. There's no cause for alarm.

PANURGE: God Almighty! So we're just two inches from death! But I'm not afraid of anything—anything but danger. (*Looking into the distance.*) Hey, there's land over there! Land ahoy!

SCENE SIX

Slyboots Island
and Physis-Antiphysis[1]

XENOMANES: That's Slyboots Island, ruled over by King Lent.

PANTAGRUEL: I've heard of him and I'd like to meet him in person.

XENOMANES: I wouldn't advise it. You wouldn't get much for your money. He's a worthy man, a devout Catholic brimming over with pardons and indulgences, but he spends nearly all his time weeping. He fasts every day, so that inside and outside he's just skin and bones. He works while doing nothing, and does nothing while he works. He nibbles suspiciously and drinks in imagination. He bathes on the tops of steeples and dries himself in ponds. . . .

PANTAGRUEL: What you say reminds me of Physis and Antiphysis.

FRIAR JOHN: And who were *they*? I've never heard of them.

(*The others gather round Pantagruel. While he is speaking his fool stands on his head.*)

PANTAGRUEL: I'll tell you.

Physis (that's another name for Nature) gave birth to Beauty and Harmony without sexual copulation.

Antiphysis, who has always been Nature's enemy, gave birth to Excess and Discord. They both had heads as round as footballs. Their ears were as big as donkeys' ears; their eyes stuck out of their heads, without eyebrows, and as hard as cankers; their feet were as round as tennis-balls; and their hands and arms turned backwards towards their shoulders.

[1] The island should not be realistically depicted. This scene should be played against a plain, abstract background.

They walked on their heads, continually turning cartwheels, arse over tit.

Antiphysis was forever praising her children and trying to prove that they were prettier than Physis's. She said that standing on your head, with your feet in the air, was imitating the Creator of the Universe, seeing that men's hairs are like roots and their legs like branches.

[Because trees are fixed more firmly in the earth by their roots than they would be by their branches. By this argument she claimed that her children were better shaped than Physis's, because they were like normal trees while Physis's were like trees upside down.]

Like that she won the admiration of every fool, every madman, every idiot, every person devoid of sound judgement and common sense. And since then she has given birth to the cretins and hypocretins, the apists and Papists, the calvinist demoniacs, the Genevan monsters, the putherbian lunatics, the toadies, humbugs, pietists, cannibals and other deformed monsters, misshapen against Nature.

CALVIN: Beast of the Apocalypse!

PUTHERBEUS: Scavenger of humanity! As dangerous in his impiety as in the scandalous nature of his writings!

CALVIN: Showing neither fear of God nor respect for men!

(*During these last speeches the ship has been becalmed. A pretty picture, full of peace and boredom. Nostalgic music.*)

SCENE SEVEN

Frozen Words[1]

XENOMANES: The wind has dropped. There's a dead calm.

CARPALIM: From port to starboard, and starboard to port. (*To*

[1] This scene should be the most poetic in the whole production.

Xenomanes.) What is Pantagruel doing, pacing up and down in front of the ship's clock?

XENOMANES: He's "passing the time of day".

CARPALIM: And what is Gymnast doing?

XENOMANES: He's dozing in his hammock with a Greek book in his hand. He believes in sleeping by the book.

CARPALIM: Eusthenes is looking through his astrolabe to find the elevation of the pole.

XENOMANES: And Friar John?

CARPALIM: He's in the galley, trying to discover what day it is from the ascendant of the spits and the horoscope of the fricassees.

XENOMANES: And Epistemon?

CARPALIM: He's day-dreaming, scratching his head with one finger and tickling himself to make himself laugh.

As for Panurge, he's smoking Pantegruelion. Look at him gargling and blowing bubbles.

(*Absolute silence.*)

PANURGE: François Villon, in his old age. . . . (*He mimes being hanged, then gives a strange laugh.*)

EPISTEMON: What a stubborn silence! Here we are, deep in thought, matragrabolized. Without saying a word to one another.

PANTAGRUEL (*suddenly getting up and listening*): Can't you hear something, friends? It seems to me that I can hear people talking in the air. But I can't see anyone. Listen!

(*Everyone listens.*)

PANURGE: I'm sniffing the air with both ears, but I can't hear anything.

GYMNAST: Open your ears as wide as oyster shells.

PANURGE: Even with my hands cupped behind them, I can't hear any voices whatever.

PANTAGRUEL: But I can hear several voices in the air, men's as well as women's.

(*A few sounds can be heard.*)

EPISTEMON: Either my ears are deceiving me, or I can hear them too.

GYMNAST: I can hear whole words.

97

PANURGE: But there's nobody there!

PANTAGRUEL: Children speaking.

EPISTEMON: Horses speaking.

(*The sounds grow louder.*)

PANURGE: God Almighty, we're done for! Let's run away! We've fallen into an ambush! Friar John, are you there, my friend?

(*The sounds grow louder still.*)

Listen! Good God, those are cannon shots! I've no courage at all at sea. Now in a cellar or anywhere else I've more than enough.

(*Diminuendo.*)

Let's run for it. There's no disgrace in running away. Demosthenes says that he who flees lives to fight another day.

PANTAGRUEL: First let's see who these people are. They may be friends of ours. Though I still can't see anybody.

(*The sounds have stopped.*)

I've read that there are several worlds touching one another and arranged in a triangle; and in the centre is the Dwelling of Truth, where there live the words, ideas, models and images of all things past and future.

I remember too that Homer's words were said to leap, fly and move about, and were consequently alive.

What is more, Plato's teaching, so they say, was like words which, when they are uttered in the depths of winter, freeze and congeal in the cold air.

May this not be the place where such words thaw out?

(*Orphic music.*)

How amazing it would be if this turned out to be the head and lyre of Orpheus!

(*The others are gathered around him like chickens under a hen's wing.*)

As you may remember, after the Thracian women had torn Orpheus to pieces, they threw his head and his lyre into the river Hebrus. They floated downstream to the sea, and then to the island of Lesbos, staying together on the waters. All the time a melancholy song issued from the head, mourning Orpheus's death: and the lyre, as the winds

plucked at its strings, played a harmonious accompaniment.
Let us look around to see if they are here.

(*Soft music.*)

XENOMANES: Milord, have no fear. Here we are at the edge of the
frozen sea, on which a great and bloody battle was fought at
the beginning of last winter. The shouts and cries of the
men and women, the clash of arms, the clanking of the
bards and harness, the neighing of the horses, and other
fearful noises of battle were frozen in the air. And now that
the rigours of winter are over, and the spring has brought
fine warm weather, they are melting so that you can hear them.

PANURGE: By God, I do believe he's right. But couldn't we see
one of them?

PANTAGRUEL (*throwing handfuls of frozen words on to the deck*):
Look, here are some that haven't thawed out yet.

(*The words start exploding.*)

They look like sugared almonds in different colours.
Red words ...
Green words ...
Blue words ...
Sable words ...
Golden words ...
Let's warm them between our hands.

(*Noises.*)

They're talking a barbarous language!
They're bursting like chestnuts thrown into a fire.

(*Cannon shots.*)

FRIAR JOHN: That was a cannon-shot.

PANURGE (*to Pantagruel*): Give me some more words, milord.

PANTAGRUEL: Only a lover gives his word.

PANURGE: Then sell me some.

PANTAGRUEL (*laughing*): Only a lawyer does that. (*He throws three
or four handfuls on to the deck. There is a positive concert of
words.*)

WORDS: Hin, hin, hin, hin, hin, hin, his, tick, tock, tack,
brededin, brededack, frr, frr, frrr, boo, boo, boo, boo, boo,
boo, boo, boo, boo, track, track, trr, trr, trr, trr, trr, on, on,
on, oo, oo, oo, oo, oo, oo, gog, magog.

99

(The sounds invade the whole theatre; neighing of horses, drums and fifes, bugles and trumpets.)

PANURGE: What if we preserved a few in oil, like snow?

PANTAGRUEL: It's folly to store up things you are never short of. . . .

PANURGE: Oh, would to God that I had the Holy Bottle's answer now, without needing to go any further!

(The sounds of battle fade away, giving place to the sound of bells, a long way off but gradually drawing nearer.)

EPISTEMON: Let's be on our way.

XENOMANES: Can you hear that noise?

PANURGE: It sounds like big bells, small bells, middle-sized bells, all ringing together.

PANTAGRUEL: It must be a swarm of bees that has taken flight, and to bring them back, the bee-keepers are banging their pots and kettles and basins. Let's put in at this island.

XENOMANES: That will give us a chance to repair our ships and stock up with provisions.

(The sound of singing.)

EPISTEMON: The singing of the inhabitants is mingling with the sound of the bells.

PANTAGRUEL: Let's go ashore.

THE ISLANDS

SCENE EIGHT
Ringing Island

They land on Ringing Island. In front of them stands the local sacristan, Aeditus, a little bald old man with a shiny red face.

PANTAGRUEL: Tell me, Father, where are we, and who lives here?

AEDITUS: This is Ringing Island. It was originally inhabited by the Siticines, but in accordance with the law of Nature, by which everything changes, they all turned into birds. (*A ballet begins, performed by birdlike monks.*)[1]

PANTAGRUEL: The cages are large, rich, luxurious, and marvellously built.

PANURGE: Anyone would think we were in Rome.

EPISTEMON: And these birds match their cages: they are big and beautiful and sleek.

PANURGE: But they look like the men in our country.

AEDITUS: Yes, they eat and drink like men, mute and fart like men, and sleep and fuck like men.

EUSTHENES: And at first sight you'd take them for men.

AEDITUS: Yet they aren't human at all.

CARPALIM: Their plumage is very odd. Some of them are all white, others all black, and others all grey. Some are half white and half black, others red, and others blue and white. What a lovely sight they make!

AEDITUS: These are the males: the clerihawks. The clerihawks give birth to priesthawks and monkhawks, without benefit of

[1] This scene is charming to begin with, but it should become sinister and eventually terrifying.

copulation. From the priesthawks come the bishhawks, and from them the beautiful cardinhawks, and if death doesn't intervene, each cardinhawk ends up as a popehawk. Usually there's only one of these, just as there's only one queen in a hive of bees, and only one sun in the sky.

PANURGE: What about the females?

AEDITUS: They are called clerikites, nunkites, priestkites, abbesskites, bishkites, cardinkites and popekites. But unfortunately we also have some bigothawks, who are like drones among bees, and who have done nothing but eat everything and spoil everything for three hundred years.

(*Putherbeus flies into a rage, thumping the arms of his throne.*)

PUTHERBEUS: He slanders all the religious orders without distinction!

PANTAGRUEL: But where do the first of these birds, the clerihawks, come from?

AEDITUS: They are all birds of passage, and they come to us from the other world. When there are too many children, male or female, in some noble house, if each received his share of the inheritance, as reason demands, Nature ordains and God commands, the estate would soon be broken up. That is why the parents get rid of their unwanted offspring on this island.

PANTAGRUEL: I'm amazed that the mothers of that world should carry their children in the womb for nine months if they can't bear them in the house for nine years, or sometimes not even seven. . . .

AEDITUS: They simply put a shirt over their clothes, cut a little hair off the tops of their heads, and after a few expiatory words turn them into the birds you see here. . . .

An even greater number come to us from Breadlessday, which is an extremely long country. For some of the inhabitants of that land find themselves starving to death and lack the skill or will to do anything, whether plying an honest trade or giving loyal service to some worthy family. Others are crossed in love, or fail in their enterprises and are driven to despair. And still others have committed some terrible crime and are in danger of death if they are caught. All of them fly here, where their livelihood is assured, and from being as thin as magpies they become as fat as dormice. Here they have perfect security, immunity and sanctuary.

FRIAR JOHN: From what country comes this horn of plenty, this abundance of good things and tasty morsels?

AEDITUS: From all parts of the other world, except for certain northern countries which a few years ago decided to "reform". But they'll rue the day they did, they will, they'll rue the day they did.

(*Calvin flies into a rage and thumps the arms of his throne.*)

CALVIN: He has abandoned the faith for materialism and irreligion.

PANTAGRUEL: Could we possibly see the Popehawk?

AEDITUS: By nature he's difficult to see. But let's steal up quietly to the cage where he's kept.

(*The Pope is seen wearing his tiara.*)

PANURGE: What has he got on his head? It looks like a tuft of feathers.

AEDITUS: Lower your voice, for God's sake. He has ears.

PANURGE: But it does look like a tuft of feathers.

AEDITUS: If he hears you blaspheming like that, you're done for, my good people.

PANTAGRUEL: Get the Popehawk to sing for us a little, so that we can hear his voice.

AEDITUS: He only sings when he feels like it.

PANTAGRUEL: I've heard that he possesses that piece of linen of Saint Veronica's.

FRIAR JOHN: Yes, the image of the Holy Face.

AEDITUS: I really can't say. In the flickering of tapers and torches, all I've ever seen on his linen is the face of a roasted rabbit!

(*Putherbeus and Calvin show their indignation by beating on their thrones.*)

CALVIN: This is insufferable!

PUTHERBEUS: By God it is! (*Surprised by his oath, he sits down again.*)

PANTAGRUEL: There's nothing to be got out of him. Let's go.

(*On their way back to the shore they meet an old green-headed bishhawk who is snoring, with a pretty white abbesskite singing happily beside him.*)

PANURGE: That pretty abbesskite is singing her heart out and that fat old bishhawk just sits there snoring. I'll make him sing, you see if I don't. (*He rings a bell which hangs above the cage.*) Wake up, you old buzzard. . . . (*He picks up a stone to throw at the bishhawk.*)

AEDITUS (*stopping him, and suddenly very stern*): My good man, strike, slay or murder all the kings and princes in the world, by treason, poison, or any other means. Or pull the angels down from their nests in the sky. For all this the Popehawk will forgive you. But never touch these sacred birds if you value your life, your fortune and your welfare—and not only yours, but those of your relatives and friends, living and dead. (*He takes leave of the terrified travellers.*)

And now let me wish you a safe journey.

One last word, my friends. You will notice that there are many more bollocks than men in this world. Bear that in mind. (*He disappears.*)

SCENE NINE

The Quavering Friars[1]

They are about to continue on their way when they notice a wall with two doors in it.

PANTAGRUEL: What is this building?

A MONK (*who was passing by*): That is the monastery built by the Quavering Friars.

EPISTEMON: In Germany they're demolishing the monasteries and defrocking the monks, but here they're putting them up.

PANURGE: Yes, but upside down and back to front.

(*A procession of Quavering Friars comes out of one door.*)

[1] This scene should be played as pure farce.

FRIAR JOHN: Look, they're dressed the wrong way round, with their cowls over their faces.

[EPISTEMON: What a pretty procession! Look at those two banners.

CARPALIM: But the banner of Fortune is being carried in front of the banner of Virtue.

PANURGE: That order is contrary to the rule laid down by Cicero and the academics, who state that Virtue must lead and Fortune follow.]

PANTAGRUEL: They are quavering very tunefully.

PANURGE: Between their teeth.

THE MONK: They only sing with their ears.

CARPALIM: Oh, what lovely music, in perfect harmony with the sound of the bells!

(*All the Friars but one go back into the monastery through the other door.*)

[PANTAGRUEL: Have you noticed how subtle these Quaverers are? Their procession came out through one door and went in through the other.

FRIAR JOHN: That's so subtle it's almost supernatural.]

PANTAGRUEL: What do these Friars do?

FRIAR JOHN: They pray to God. All in quavers.

THE MONK: And sing through their ears, as I've explained.

PANURGE: And when do they play the two-backed beast, I'd like to know? (*To the Quavering Friar who has stayed behind.*) Friar Quaver, or Semiquaver, where's the girl?

FRIAR (*pointing to the wall*): There.

PANURGE: Have you got many in there?

FRIAR: Few.

PANURGE: But how many exactly?

FRIAR: Five.

PANURGE: And how many would you like?

FRIAR: Ten.

PANURGE: Where do you hide them?

FRIAR: Here.

PANURGE: What sort of figures do they have?

FRIAR: Good.

PANURGE: What are their complexions like?

FRIAR: Clear.
PANURGE: Their hair?
FRIAR: Fair.
PANURGE: Their eyes?
FRIAR: Black.
PANURGE: Their tits?
FRIAR: Round.
PANURGE: Their features?
FRIAR: Fine.
PANURGE: Their eyebrows?
FRIAR: Smooth.
PANURGE: Their charms?
FRIAR: Ripe.
PANURGE: Their gaze?
FRIAR: Frank.
PANURGE: Their feet?
FRIAR: Flat.
PANURGE: Their arms?
FRIAR: Long.
PANURGE: How do you feed them?
FRIAR: Well.
PANURGE: What do they eat?
FRIAR: Bread.
PANURGE: What sort of bread?
FRIAR: Brown.
PANURGE: And what else?
FRIAR: Meat.
PANURGE: How do they eat it?
FRIAR: Roast.
PANURGE: Do they eat any fish?
FRIAR: Yes.
PANURGE: And what else?
FRIAR: Eggs.
PANURGE: How do they like them?
FRIAR: Boiled.
PANURGE: Boiled in what way?
FRIAR: Hard.
PANURGE: And what do they drink?

FRIAR: Lots.

PANURGE: Lots of what?

FRIAR: Wine.

PANURGE: What sort of wine?

FRIAR: White.

PANURGE: What a delightful fellow this Quaverer is! Would to God he were the Chief Justice of the Paris court! By God, what a shortener of cases and resolver of disputes he'd make! But let's go back to our little sisters of charity. (*To the Friar.*) When you take your pleasure with them, what are their pharmacopoeias like?

FRIAR: Big.

PANURGE: And the entrance?

FRIAR: Fresh.

PANURGE: And inside?

FRIAR: Deep.

PANURGE: What's the temperature?

FRIAR: Warm.

PANURGE: And what's on the outside?

FRIAR: Hair.

PANURGE: Of what colour?

FRIAR: Red.

PANURGE: And of the older ones?

FRIAR: Grey.

PANURGE: And what's the sacking of them like?

FRIAR: Quick.

PANURGE: Their buttock-play?

FRIAR: Brisk.

PANURGE: Would you like them to wriggle more?

FRIAR: Less.

PANURGE: And what are your tools like?

FRIAR: Large.

PANURGE: And in section?

FRIAR: Round.

PANURGE: What colour at the end?

FRIAR: Pink.

PANURGE: When they've finished, what are they like?

FRIAR: Shrunk.

PANURGE: And how would you describe your balls?

FRIAR: Huge.

PANURGE: Now, by the oath you've taken, when you want to cover them, how do you lay them?

FRIAR: Down.

PANURGE: What do they say when you fuck them?

FRIAR: Nowt.

PANURGE: Do they bear you any children?

FRIAR: None.

PANURGE: How do you lie together?

FRIAR: Bare.

PANURGE: Again by that oath you've taken, how many times a day do you usually do it?

FRIAR: Six.

PANURGE: And how many times a night?

FRIAR: Ten.

FRIAR JOHN: A pox on it, the poor fellow sticks at fourteen. He must be bashful.

PANURGE: Come now, Friar John, could you do as well as that? (*To the Friar.*) But do the others do it as much as that?

FRIAR: All.

PANURGE: And who's the cock of the walk?

FRIAR: I.

PANURGE: Have you ever served a fault?

FRIAR: Nay.

PANURGE: But if by some lawful impediment there occurs some diminution of the member, how do you feel then?

FRIAR: Bad.

PANURGE: And what do the girls do?

FRIAR: Curse.

PANURGE: What do you give them?

FRIAR: Thwacks.

PANURGE: So that you are always . . .

FRIAR: Feared.

PANURGE: And they take you for . . .

FRIAR: Saints.

PANURGE: By God, I like this poor Quaverer. I think I'll take

108

him home with me, and when I'm married he can serve my wife as a fool.

EPISTEMON: He'll serve your wife all right, but you'll be the fool. (*The Friar leaves.*)

PUTHERBEUS: What a disgrace to good morals and public decency!

CALVIN: He deserves condemnation!

SCENE TEN

The Furry Cats

The sky darkens. The lighting becomes sinister.

PANTAGRUEL: Where are we now, and what's this desert island?

XENOMANES: This is Condemnation.

PANURGE: Let's piss off quick.

PANTAGRUEL: And the next island?

XENOMANES: That's the Wicket. But I don't advise you to go there, for we might be arrested.

PANTAGRUEL: Who lives there?

XENOMANES: The Furry Cats, horrible, frightening creatures, who eat little children and feed on marble slabs—just like those in the Palace of Justice in Paris.

Their badge and symbol is an open game-bag. They have long, strong claws which are very sharp, and nothing can escape their clutches.

(*Suddenly the atmosphere becomes very Kafkaesque. The Beggar stands before them. A large notice hangs over the stage, bearing the words: PALACE OF JUSTICE.*)

THE BEGGAR (*in tragic tones*): Good people, God grant that you may get out of here. For soon, under Grimalkin justice, you'll see the Furry Cats lords of all Europe. They seize everything, devour everything, beshit everything. They burn, quarter, behead, imprison, ruin and undermine everything, without any distinction between good and bad.

Among them vice is called virtue, wickedness is entitled goodness, treason bears the name of loyalty, and theft is styled generosity. Plunder is their motto. And if ever plagues, famines or wars, storms, cataclysms or conflagrations, or any other misfortunes afflict the world, do not attribute them to the conjunctions of the planets, to the tyranny of kings, to the imposture of hypocrites, heretics and false prophets, to the ignorance of doctors, or to the perversity of adulterous women. Attribute them all to the enormous, unspeakable, incredible, inestimable wickedness of the Furry Cats.

PANURGE: By God, if it's like that, I'm not going in there! Let's turn back, for God's sake! This worthy beggar has given me a bigger scare than thunder in autumn.

(*A sudden clap of thunder. A gate closes and Grimalkin appears. He is a fantastic creature, part lion, part dog, part wolf and part dragon. Rays of light shine all around him. Beside him sits Grimalkin Justice, an old woman wearing spectacles. In place of the scales of justice, she is holding in her left hand two game-bags, one full of bullion and hanging down, and the other high up and empty. In her right hand she is holding a sickle.*)

THE BEGGAR: That's Grimalkin and his wife, Grimalkin Justice.

GRIMALKIN: Be seated!

PANURGE (*trembling*): Thank you very much, but I'm all right as I am.

GRIMALKIN: Sit down there, and don't let us have to tell you again. The earth will open up and swallow you all alive if you fail to answer our questions properly. (*In a hoarse, angry voice.*) Come now, come now, come now.
(*Everyone sits down.*)

PANURGE (*between his teeth*): I could do with a drink now!

GRIMALKIN: Come now, answer this riddle:
A pretty young maiden as fair as may be
Without help from a man had a coal black babee,
And strange to relate, no birthpains did gripe her,
Though the child in his haste gnawed her side like a viper.

Come now, solve that for me straight away. Come now,
hurry up!

PANURGE: By God now, if I had a Sphinx at home, I could
solve your riddle. But by God now, I wasn't there, and by
God now, I'm not guilty.

GRIMALKIN: Come now, you villain, so you plead not guilty, do
you, as if that were enough to save you from our tortures.
Come now, our laws are like spiders' webs. Little gnats and
butterflies get caught in them, but as for the big poisonous
horseflies, come now, they break them now and pass through
them now. By the same token now, we don't look for the
big thieves and tyrants. Come now, they're too hard to
digest, and they'd hurt us if we swallowed them now.

But as for you little innocents, come now, the great devil
shall sing a Mass for you now.

FRIAR JOHN (*put out of patience by Grimalkin's speech*): Come
now, Master Devil-in-robes, how can you expect him to
answer in a case he knows nothing about? Aren't you
satisfied with the truth?

GRIMALKIN: Come now, this is the first time in my reign that
anyone has spoken here without being questioned first.
Come now, who has let this madman loose on us?

FRIAR JOHN (*between his teeth*): You're a liar.

GRIMALKIN: Come now, you'll have enough on your hands when
its your turn to answer.

FRIAR JOHN (*between his teeth*): Yes, you scoundrel, you're a liar.

GRIMALKIN: Come now, here you have to answer now what you
don't know. Here you confess now to what you've done,
when you've never done it. Here you swear now you know
what you've never learnt. (*To Panurge.*) Come now, come
now, stupid, aren't you going to say anything?

PANURGE: By the devil now, I can see the plague's upon us now,
seeing that innocence isn't safe now, and the devil says his
Mass now, devil take it now. So I beg you to let me go bail
now for everyone now, and by the devil now, let us go
now.

GRIMALKIN: Let you go? Come now, in three hundred years now,
nobody has ever escaped from here now without leaving

something behind now, if he hasn't solved the riddle now. Come now, what does it mean now?

PANURGE: The fair maiden and her black baby? Come now, it means a black weevil now, born of a white bean now, through the hole now, it had gnawed now. Just as in this life now, you gnaw away and eat up everything. (*Panurge flings into the middle of the courtroom a great purse full of sun crowns.*)

THE FURRY CATS: These are the sweets of justice! It's been a good case, a tasty case, a spicy case. And these are worthy people.

PANURGE: Come now, that's gold now.

GRIMALKIN: Come now, the Court appreciates that. So come now, you may go now.

(*Taxalot appears on the left-hand platform.*)

EPISTEMON: Those people could get oil from a stone.

XENOMANES: They could and they do. And so does that fellow over there. (*He points to Taxalot.*)

PANTAGRUEL: What is his name?

XENOMANES: Taxalot. He keeps the accounts at the Audit Office. That's where they squeeze everything in the great Treasury Press: castles, parks, forests, fortifications, estates, pleasures, posts, offerings, the Royal Household, and even the people's savings, the best vine in the country.

EPISTEMON: And what is that great Treasury Press made of?

XENOMANES: It's made from the wood of the Cross. The screw is called *receipts*, the bowl *expenditure*, the vice *the State*, and the funnel *value added*.

PANTAGRUEL: By virtue of what right?

XENOMANES: No right or reason, except their Lordships' instructions, their Lordships' wishes, their Lordships' orders.

(*Grimalkin has remained in his seat. Aeditus has come back with a bird beside him. The Quavering Friar on the right-hand platform, Taxalot on the left-hand platform.*)

PANTAGRUEL (*pointing to these four "dangers" and making a sort of sign of the Cross*): The Church, Justice, Indulgences and the Treasury.

God be praised for having delivered us from such great danger.

(*Thunder and lightning. The stage is plunged into darkness.*)

SCENE ELEVEN
Ship of Fools

ORATOR: But the danger is still there, despite the protection of
  Coligny and the De Guises, and the kindness of Henri II
  and Diane de Poitiers.

    The Faculty of Theology condemns him out of hand.
  Some of the friends of his youth are on the jury. . . .
  Henceforth he takes care to give no sign of life.
  He resigns the livings of Jambet and Meudon.
  It is rumoured that he is in prison.
  The voyage continues in the dark.[1]

    (*The travellers are once again at sea. They meet another ship,
  which seems to wish to come alongside (see Hieronymus Bosch's*
  Ship of Fools).)

GYMNAST: Ahoy there! A ship full of monks to starboard!

ALL: Jacobins, Capuchins, Franciscans, Theatins!

PANURGE: Greetings, blessed fathers! Where do you come from?

THE MONKS: Council of Chesil!

PANURGE: Council of Fools?

THE MONKS: Council of Trent!

GYMNAST: What did you do there?

THE MONKS: Sifted the articles of Faith and burned the new
  heretics!

PANURGE: The deviationists? Burning one of those brings you
  luck for the rest of the day. I commend the salvation of my
  soul to your pious prayers.

THE MONKS: But what about you? Have you seen him?

PANTAGRUEL: Whom?

[1] The reign of François I was under the sign of the Sun. During the reign
of Henri II the Moon of Diane de Poitiers was in the ascendant.

THE MONKS: The One and Only!

EPISTEMON: One and only what?

THE MONKS: He who is. Have you ever seen him?

PANTAGRUEL: He who is, is God. And he isn't visible to earthly eyes.

THE MONKS: We don't mean God in Heaven. We mean God on earth. Have you seen him?

CARPALIM: Upon my honour, they mean the Pope!

PANURGE: Why yes, gentlemen, I've seen three of them, but only one at a time! And seeing the Pope has never done me the slightest bit of good.

(The ship disappears. Pantagruel's ship continues on its way. Crystalline music. A light appears, then several more. They seem to be playing together.)

GYMNAST: Look at those little lights moving over the sea!

PANTAGRUEL: I think they must be fiery fishes.

XENOMANES: No, those are the watchlights of Lanternland. We shall be entering the harbour in a few moments.

(All sorts of lanterns appear, creating a magical effect. The ship is moored.)

EPISTEMON: The people here live on nothing but lanterns. Demosthenes came here once in search of illumination, but afterwards his speeches all smelled of midnight oil.

LIGHTGUARD: Explain the purpose of your visit.

PANTAGRUEL: We have come to ask the Queen of Lanternland for a Lantern to light us and guide us to the Oracle of the Bottle.

LIGHTGUARD: You have come at a good time, for the Lanterns are holding their Provincial Chapter just now, and you'll have a good choice. Lantern of Aristophanes, take them to the palace. *(As they leave.)*

PANURGE *(frisking about)*: At last we've found what we've been looking for, after all that toil and trouble!

SCENE TWELVE
Lanternland[1]

Lanternland. The Temple of the Holy Bottle. Enter, all half-naked (recalling Diane de Poitiers): The Queen of Lanternland; Princess Bacbuc; the Company of Lanterns and Lamps (the latter wearing phallic costumes); and young Bacchus. A projector is used to show the triumph of Bacchus. During the introductory ballet, which should last about three minutes, the recorded conversation of the travellers is played while they are approaching the stage.

A VOICE (*echoing*): As you pass the postern, pray
    Let a lantern light your way.
EPISTEMON: Oh, what a splendid temple!
XENOMANES: Look at the incredible battle good old Bacchus won
    over the Indians.
PANTAGRUEL: With Silenus in the vanguard, bent, plump and
    paunchy. . . .
CARPALIM: . . . accompanied by his young satyrs. . . .
EUSTHENES: . . . all naked, dancing and jumping. . . .
PANURGE: . . . leaping and prancing, farting and kicking. . . .
FRIAR JOHN: . . . with tails and horns like young goats. . . .
EPISTEMON: . . . and surrounded by naked women.
PANTAGRUEL: And Bacchus in the middle.

[1] This scene should be fantastic, surrealistic. Everything about it should be crystalline, sparkling, erotic. The mood should work up to a dionysiac frenzy.

PANURGE: He looks like a child.

FRIAR JOHN: Because good drinkers never grow old.

ALL: *Evohé!*

(*The dance continues.*)

THE VOICE (*echoing*): The Fates lead him who consents and drag him who refuses.

(*While Pantagruel, Panurge, Friar John and Epistemon are coming on stage.*)

PLAY-LEADER (*commenting on the setting*): And here is the wonderful lamp, made entirely of precious stones: amethysts, carbuncles, rubies and opals. And the fantastic Fountain.

(*The ballet ends in a final frenzy. Silence. The women become aware of the presence of the four visitors.*)

PANURGE: What pleasant, joyous company!

FIRST LANTERN: Be of good hope and whatever you see, have no fear.

(*They approach her timidly.*)

PANURGE: This reminds me of the painted cellar in Chinon.

PANTAGRUEL: I know Chinon: a little city of great renown.

FRIAR JOHN: I've drunk many a glass of fresh wine there. (*A Lantern brushes against him.*) Horny horniculture!

SECOND LANTERN: Put vine-leaves in your shoes and hold a green branch in your left hand.

PANTAGRUEL: Thyrsus in hand.

THIRD LANTERN: Each of you make an Albanian hat of this ivy and put it on.

THE QUEEN: There is a mystical reason for what we ask.

FIRST LANTERN: Friends, follow the instructions of Princess Bacbuc.

(*They reach the centre of the stage and gather around the fountain, a thin jet of water.*)

BACBUC: Do us the favour of drinking from this fountain. But first listen to the sound of the water.

THE TRAVELLERS: Water?

BACBUC: Drink it. (*They finally drink.*) Now tell me what you think of it.

PANTAGRUEL: It tastes like good fresh spring-water, clear and silvery. . . .

BACBUC: Pilgrims, are your throats so caked, paved and enamelled that you fail to recognize the taste or savour of this divine liquor? (*To her ladies-in-waiting*. Bring here those scourers of mine to rake, clear and clean their palates. (*The ladies-in-waiting bring in hams, saveloys, sausages, etc. While they are eating.*)

Once upon a time, when Moses was leading his people across the desert, he asked Heaven for manna, and to their imagination it tasted just like food. In the same way, here, drinking this wonderful liquor, you will recognize the taste of whatever wine you choose to imagine. So imagine and drink. (*They drink again.*)

PANURGE: By God, this is Beaune wine!

FRIAR JOHN: By my faith as a Lanterner, it's Graves wine, gay and sparkling.

PANTAGRUEL: To me it seems like Mirevaux wine, for that's what I imagined it to be.

VOICE (*recorded*): In Wine is Truth.
(*The guests drink greedily.*)

BACBUC: Imagine another wine, and drink again. You will find the taste and savour of the liquor just as you imagined it. And confess that to God nothing is impossible.

FRIAR JOHN: He is all-powerful.

BACBUC: Which of you wishes to consult the Holy Bottle?

PANURGE: I, your humble little funnel.

[BACBUC: Let him be dressed.[1]

(*Music. Panurge's face is washed three times and daubed with flour. He is made to dance, jump in the air, and bump his bottom on the ground. The Queen of Lanternland has picked up a bottle and is dancing round the fountain. The "magical" ceremony begins with a recorded incantation by Bacbuc.*)
(*She murmurs during the preparations.*)

Bathe his face three times,
Flour in his eyes,
A feather in his hair,
Dance,
Jump,
Arse on the ground.

[1] This text was omitted from the Élysée-Montmartre production. It would have been drowned by the incantatory music.

O
Bottle Full
Of mystery
With one ear
I hark to thee
Do not delay
But quickly say
The word I crave
My life to save
For within your flanks divine
Bacchus, the noble god of wine
Keeps the solemn word concealed
Which by you may be revealed.
I hark and wait,
Pray speak my fate.
O Bottle full
Of mystery.]

(*The music rises to a climax. The dance becomes wilder. Panurge, like Buster Keaton in a voodoo ceremony, is completely possessed. The noise grows louder and finally explodes in one word.*)

TRINK!

(*The Queen freezes. Panurge is on his knees in front of her.*)

PANURGE: God Almighty, it's cracked.

BACBUC: Friend, give thanks to the gods. You have heard the answer of the Bottle, the most joyous and divine answer I have ever heard.

The philosophers of your world feed you with words through the ears. Here we administer our teaching through the mouth. (*She hands him a flask in the shape of a breviary.*)

I do not tell you: "Read this chapter, study that gloss." I tell you: "Taste this chapter, swallow that gloss." (*He drinks.*)

The word *Trink* is understood by all nations. It means: Drink.

In wine is truth.

In wine is life, strength, and power.

Drink of life.

Be your own judge of what you do.

To reach the end of the road of knowledge, take God as your guide and man as your companion.

Drink of life.

(*Frenzied music. Everyone dances . . . a modern dance. The women dance around Panurge, who goes into a positive ecstasy. During the dance.*)

FRIAR JOHN (*recorded*): He's bewitched! . . . He's foaming at the mouth! . . . His eyes are rolling like a dying goat's!

(*Suddenly Panurge falls to the ground. The music stops dead. The women run away. A change of lighting.*)

EPILOGUE

The Death of Rabelais

We are in the Present, on the stage of a modern theatre. It is not clear whether the dying man on the stage is Rabelais or the actor playing Panurge. The others gather round him and take off his costume, so that the human being can no longer be situated in time. Young Bacchus, standing alone a little way off, gazes at him.

THE DYING MAN: I haven't a penny, I owe a lot, I give the rest to the poor.

PIERRE AMY, THE PLAY-LEADER: Here on the boards lies Rabelais, whose sharp nose stung the sharpest stingers.

THE DYING MAN (*panting for breath*): The Sacrament! (*The Play-Leader holds out his microphone.*) Grease my boots for the great journey.

ORATOR: Even as he lay dying he made fun of those who showed concern over his death.

RABELAIS (*to Pierre Amy*): I am going in search of a great Perhaps. (*A man goes by with some doves.*) Friend, where do those doves come from?

THE MAN: Sir, they come from the *other world*. Whenever life here opens up, they come by.

(*Silence. He breathes heavily. A few doves peck at the ground around him. Then with a last smile he says.*)

RABELAIS: Ring down the curtain, the farce is over.

(*Silence. Darkness falls on Panurge while a huge portrait of Rabelais is lit up.*)

January-May 1968